HOW
GOOGLE TO
SELL SAMOSAS

Praise for *How I Quit Google to Sell Samosas*

'This book made me cry, laugh and feel hungry all at the same time.'

—Farah Khan, filmmaker

'Love for your values, respect for your culture, entrepreneurial spirit to give it life. Read the book to find out more!'

—Vikas Agnihotri, former managing director, Google India, and operating partner, SoftBank Investment Advisers

'I'm an admirer of Munaf's audacity and ambition. As a fellow "solopreneur", I can relate to his bumpy but always joyous journey. There is much to learn here!'

—Anupama Chopra, film critic and author

'Munaf stands for everything I wish I had done when I was his age. His food journey inspires me, and I am sure it will inspire you as well.'

—Ranveer Brar, chef, TV show host, and author of *Come into My Kitchen*

'As an entrepreneur in the food business I could relate to Munaf's stories and experiences. I love how honest, real AND inspiring his narrative is—from giving up a coveted job, the many highs and lows of the business to the realities of a deadly pandemic. I'm sure any budding entrepreneur would find value and encouragement by reading Munaf's story.'

—Pooja Dhingra, owner, Le15 Patisserie, and author of *The Big Book of Treats*

'I have huge respect for the way Munaf created a delicious experience at home with his family serving Bohra food, then branded it as The Bohri Kitchen and marketed it brilliantly to make it the success it is today. He is a case study and inspiration for so many looking to enter this industry with their own ideas.'

—AD Singh, founder and managing director, Olive Group of Restaurants

'Munaf's madness, combined with his mother's love for home-style Bohra food, are the perfect recipe for a journey worth taking.'

—Sanjeev Kapoor, chef, author and TV personality

'Persistence always goes a long way! Munaf believed in what he wanted and didn't shy away from following his passion. His stories are not only engaging, they are also inspiring. All of us have experienced the same struggles as Munaf at some point or other and his account of them will resonate with anyone from the hospitality industry.'

—Riyaaz Amlani, CEO and MD, Impresario Entertainment & Hospitality Pvt. Ltd

'The book is an exhilarating and honest account of Munaf's life. It's not just a great weekend read, but a story that shows us the power of belief, the importance of persistence and that life is what we make of it. It will inspire you to stand up and do something—and do it NOW! I congratulate Munaf for being so forthcoming about his entire journey, including speaking about his failures so candidly. I am definitely inspired, and I hope many more people read this book and go on to help build the country through great ideas and entrepreneurship.'

—Saurabh Kalra, COO, McDonald's India (West and South)

'One hears of catchwords like grit, persistence, ambition and passion in many a success story. I have seen them come together in human form in Munaf. He had an insight, built an idea around it and pursued it to the point of going broke. But passion is the best motivator. This book is about inspiration, guts, and the dream to be the best. This is just the beginning of his story.'

—**Sunil Lulla, CEO, Broadcast Audience Research Council, India**

'How do you successfully convert a great idea into reality … read this book.'

—**Satish Mathur, former director general of police, Maharashtra**

'This is a book about a unique journey, not a rags-to-riches story! It's the story of a spiritual journey, a passage to find the truth within one's heart.'

—**Prahlad Kakar, a man with many hats**

'As Munaf has said, entrepreneurship by definition is a marathon. His story shows how we should always follow our dreams and, despite all the twists and turns, keep believing and finally, stay resilient.'

—**Bahram N. Vakil, founding partner, AZB & Partners**

'As I progressed through the book it just reinforced the fact that Munaf as always, tells a great story. A story of stepping out of the relative safety net that a global corporate provides. A story of the journey of entrepreneurship and building a brand from the ground up. A story of grit and the determination to pursue a dream. Read it carefully enough and you'll find some endearing lessons for life.'

—**Romil Ratra, executive director and CEO, Graviss Hospitality**

HOW I QUIT GOOGLE TO SELL SAMOSAS

ADVENTURES WITH THE BOHRI KITCHEN

MUNAF KAPADIA

WITH ZAHABIA RAJKOTWALA

HarperCollins *Publishers* India

First published by
HarperCollins *Publishers* in 2021
A-75, Sector 57, Noida, Uttar Pradesh 201301, India
www.harpercollins.co.in

2 4 6 8 10 9 7 5 3 1

P-ISBN: 978-93-5422-257-3
E-ISBN: 978-93-5422-258-0

Typeset in 11.5/15 Minion Pro at
Manipal Technologies Limited, Manipal

Printed and bound at
Thomson Press (India) Ltd.

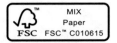

For my parents, Nafisa and Turab Kapadia, without whom there would be no TBK.

My wife, Zahabia Rajkotwala—without you there would be no book.

For the Indian housewife, who remains the most precious yet underacknowledged asset our country has. Thank you, from the bottom of my heart, for being the last custodian of our cuisine and tradition.

Contents

Foreword

'First-of-its-kind! … memorable …' not only describes my finger-licking, shortcut-to-bliss meal at Munaf Kapadia's The Bohri Kitchen, but also this book that you are holding in your hands. In fact, this book is as much of a multidimensional extravaganza as my three-hour-long, eight-course, guilt-free, non-stop thaal lunch. It was a taste of Dawoodi Bohra culture, an exciting commentary on the rare ingredients and their cooking and eating customs. As is this book. It's more … much more.

My introduction to the Munaf magic was all thanks to my friend Rishi Kapoor, the gourmet of all gourmets, the high-octane, award-winning charismatic actor who had four generations of film and foodie genes. I write this with gratitude to Rishi—it's thanks to his passion and gourmet gusto that I discovered The Bohri Kitchen and shared the experience in my *Bombay Times* column, on social media, and even created a Bohri food award category for the Times Food Awards (now Times Food and Nightlife Awards).

And now, it gives me equal joy to share this book. The catchy title, *How I Quit Google to Sell Samosas*, does not even begin to express the multi-course thaal of messages that the book serves up.

A riveting personal story

It's a family saga. The cook is the mom (Nafisa), the head of operations is the father (Turab) and the CEO (Chief Eating Officer) is the son Munaf.

Munaf, one of four siblings, inherited his father's entrepreneurial genes. His father built his business from the ground up, eventually buying out a wholesale business from Munaf's grandfather. From competing with three hundred candidates vying for a coveted, client-facing role at Google's New Delhi and Mumbai offices to almost being fired from the company, Munaf displayed tremendous entrepreneurial spirit in the initial years. Quite clearly, the job as an account strategist wasn't cutting it, even if it was—in his own words—the best company in the world to work for. His life story is an inspirational one for those mired in a nine-to-five job and looking to unleash their entrepreneurial spirit.

Motivational masala

Munaf stirs into his food story, motivational masala for budding entrepreneurs. All the hazards, the ups and down, loans, home dining experiences to delivery kitchens to raising private equity are honestly and impeccably recorded. It's a brilliant blueprint for all start-ups.

The food story unravels, just like the alternating courses of kharaas-meethas (savoury-sweet) in our leisurely lunch. It's sprinkled with humour, too.

From taxes to tacos

Call it serendipity! Call it synchronicity! But it all comes together in a sublimely delicious way. My life story is on the same lines as 'Google to Samosas' except that mine is from 'Taxes to Tacos'. Having qualified as a journalist from Bombay University, I went on to write the IAS exam and, through my days with the Income Tax Department in Mumbai, continued to explore the city through its restaurants. And write about them.

When I quit the Income Tax Department to start a weekly column in *The Bombay Times* and do TV shows, I was criticized for quitting a powerful job to write about brownies. Just like Munaf was. Food writing was not fashionable then and there was no internet. I wrote India's first-ever city restaurant guide, and it went on to become a national bestseller. Though I've written over forty books and hosted many a food show since, I've never had to face the entrepreneur's dilemmas that Munaf dealt—and continues to deal—with. Kudos to him for keeping his head above water.

All through my writing career, my passion has always been the home chef. Over thirty years ago, when I started my column in *The Bombay Times*, I insisted on an answering machine for readers to call in and share their home chef favourites. It thrills me to no end that, with

TBK, Munaf bridges the gap—between a home chef and restaurateur—brilliantly, serving up not only a unique, memorable experience but also this magnificent multi-course book which you are now holding in your hands.

Turn the pages. Go on. What are you waiting for?

24 February 2021   **Rashmi Uday Singh**

1

The Day I Quit Google

It happened quite unexpectedly.

I remember the date—15 June 2015. The months leading up to it had been a seismic period for me, professionally. After four years with Google India, in Hyderabad and then Mumbai, I was contemplating a move within the company to one of their many foreign offices.

In those months, I'd found myself battling this inexplicable feeling, one that had led me to quit my previous job. I couldn't stop thinking that my current role at Google, that once had me burning the midnight oil, now took up less than half my office hours.

Vikas Agnihotri, my super boss[1], pulled me into one of the conference rooms at the Mumbai office. He sat me down and said, 'We've heard a lot about The Bohri Kitchen,

---

[1] Vikas Agnihotri subsequently went on to become the head of Google India. He is currently India's first Operating Partner at SoftBank Investment Advisers.

Munaf, and we want to know what you have planned for its future.'

I was caught off guard. I'm sure you are too. What is The Bohri Kitchen, and why did my super boss concern himself with it?

An hour later, I made the fateful decision to quit Google.

The story of how I quit Google begins at the end of the 2010 placement season at Mumbai's Narsee Monjee Institute of Management Studies (NMIMS). Along with twenty other students, I had spent countless hours over two months in freezing cold, air-conditioned classrooms, waiting to be interviewed by company reps. The dull white lights in the old MBA building cast a gloom over the recruitment process, cranking up our anxiety levels by several notches (the new structure, which resembles an airport hangar, was still under construction). Every candidate went through a couple of interviews followed by a moderated group discussion with competing candidates. The selection criteria were simple—did you possess the technical know-how for the job? (And in case you didn't, were you at least smart enough to be trained for the job?) Did you play well with others? (An assessment of your leadership and managerial skills.) Did you have passable communication skills? (Inevitably, most of us needed assistance in this area after joining. Business emails are TUFF!)

Everyone in business school had stars in their eyes when they saw a future as a management trainee at a multinational company ('FMCG MNC'). Getting placed at a Hindustan Unilever (HUL) or Procter & Gamble (P&G) is what dreams were made of for us dewy, blazer-donning, MBA grads. Very few of us knew what *really* motivated us. I mean, yes, some of us liked marketing, others enjoyed numbers (so maybe, finance?); then, there were the rare few who were drawn to human resources (HR) and the crazy ones who considered advertising! What any of this actually meant in terms of real work, and whether we would enjoy it, well, I'm not sure if anyone had any clarity there. We still had to pretend we did to bag the job, though! *Fake it till you make it.*

By the summer of 2011, I had graduated from NMIMS's MBA in Marketing Management programme and secured a placement as management trainee at Wrigley India Pvt. Ltd. (a Mars company). I was officially in the business of selling chewing gum.

The role was an incredible opportunity for me to grasp the ground realities of an FMCG (fast-moving consumer goods) business before assuming a managerial position in its sales hierarchy. More importantly, for the first time ever, I got a taste of life away from home. All the trainees who were part of Wrigley's summer intake that year attended an orientation programme in Gurgaon where we were also allocated our respective assignments for the quarter. Then, like a vigorously shuffled deck of cards, we were evenly distributed across the North, South, East and West of India. I was stationed south in rural Mysore (now Mysuru), Karnataka, to shadow a regional sales officer whose name was Lingaraju. I was tasked with learning the ways of chewing gum selling and reporting back to the head office with my insights and recommendations.

My stint in Mysore with Wrigley often felt like an expedition on *The Amazing Race*. I had no understanding of the regional tongue, Kannada, or any idea of how to find my way around this remote region! Lingaraju doubled up as both Phil Keoghan[2] and my teammate, assigning me tasks on one hand ('sell gum') and helping me complete them on the other ('bribe retailers with a bucket to display your gum'). He also threw in useful tips on where to eat and shop, and sightseeing in the vicinity.

Three months in Mysore taught me many things about myself and the job at hand. It also taught me that Lingaraju could climb a coconut tree, secure the fruit and climb down in under a minute[3]. But perhaps the most important thing

---

2   Phil Keoghan is the renowned host of *The Amazing Race* series and has been with the show since its inception in 2001.

3   Meeting Lingaraju is the best memory I have of my Mysore experience. In the few days we spent together, we became really tight. He invited me into his home and his family plied me with freshly cooked mango rice and dal. It was amazing to see small-town life from his point of view, strengthening my impression that south India is definitely superior in terms of gender balance, literacy and safety as compared to other parts of India. The most remarkable thing about my visit to Lingaraju's home, though, had to be a cow sitting in his living room!

I learnt is that I needed to genuinely believe in a product if I'm going to try and sell it.

Despite all the fun and games, as the weeks wore on, I found myself getting increasingly restless. At Wrigley, I was one among four trainees on the fast track to becoming an area manager. I was getting paid exceptionally well, living by myself across the country and was on a high-flying, corporate career track. I thought this would be the year that I turned into that independent, ambitious, bright-eyed, twenty-two-year-old protagonist you see in Hollywood coming-of-age movies. (Ironically, almost eight years later, I'm still very much living with my parents and continue to exploit their hospitality shamelessly.)

While Wrigley probably sells the best chewing gum out there, it wasn't *sticky* enough for me to endure sleepless nights poring over sales targets or frequent rotations in different parts of the country.

In hindsight, I can see that I've always had an issue with a conventional sales role.

Till date, my father narrates the story of my placement interview with a leading tobacco company, which I happened to ace. But when the interviewer asked me, 'Munaf, how would you feel working for a company that is selling a product that kills lakhs every year,' I had no response. I realized I couldn't do it and asked if I could use my humble talents to sell their biscuits instead!

For me, it's more than just achieving a target—it's also about evangelism and education. I needed a brand, a product or a service which I could truly evangelize.

As an employer today, I am always wary when it comes to hiring freshers because if there's one thing my Wrigley experience taught me, it's that *your first job gets you ready for the next one.* Management schools don't do enough to draw out your professional strengths and weaknesses. But your first job does that to a great extent. You accept the role, praying to God (or whatever else gets you going) that you've done right by yourself and your employer. When you finally spend time earning that pay cheque, sitting down for appraisals and considering the possibility that this might be five-seventh of your life, you are inwardly compelled to evaluate what *really* motivates you and activates those creative juices.

As luck would have it, three months into my time at Wrigley, I got a call from the recruiters at Google India, to interview for a position at their Hyderabad office.

I was conflicted about job-hopping this early in my career. I had barely spent any time on my first assignment at Wrigley, so quitting now felt impulsive. I had no real complaints here; in fact, the leadership had put together a genuinely good management trainee programme with a goal to shape us into skilled executives. But the lure of working for a tech giant with roots in Silicon Valley was irresistible. I could also blame what happened next on *the-grass-is-always-greener-on-the-other-side* syndrome. In this instance, making the decision to interview with Google put me on a path that made no logical sense, career or growth-wise, but turned out to be *the* best decision I have ever made in my life.

The first time I visited the Google campus in HITEC City, Hyderabad, I was mesmerized. They had leased an entire building—ten storeys high—with a gleaming glass facade. Walking from the main entrance to the lobby, you pass a massive cafeteria on the ground floor. Enclosed by floor-to-ceiling glass, visitors are offered a glimpse of hundreds of Googlers browsing an almost-infinite number of culinary options. (I often wonder whether the decision I made four years later to become a food entrepreneur was influenced by the gastronomic experiences I had at Google!)

As I walked past the cafeteria, I fell in love with what I saw—Googlers. I felt an energy that one experiences on a college campus—one that is young and vibrant, enhanced by individuals with stellar IQs, winning personalities and a genuine passion for what they do. It was evident that every person on that campus was the best in class for their role at Google. I was already excited to interact with and learn from them.

The path to becoming a 'Noogler'[4] wasn't smooth. I survived three rigorous rounds of interviews while I was still working at Wrigley and living in Mysore.

Then came what was to be my very first pay negotiation with Google HR. They had offered me a position (yay!) but

---

4   New Googlers or freshers are called Nooglers on Google campuses, the world over.

at a forty per cent pay cut (nay!) from what I was making at Wrigley.

When I asked them to reconsider, I received this polite response: 'We are sorry we can't match your expectations right now, but you can always apply again next year.' Like hell! I signed my employment contract with Google the very next day. I haven't seen a more effective use of reverse psychology ever since.

The roadblocks didn't end here, however. I had to tactfully and patiently convince my parents that this sudden decision to quit a well-paying job at a multinational company within three months of joining wasn't me having a meltdown. At first, they were convinced that I was being short-sighted, probably overwhelmed or just plain scared by what real employment and hard work looked like.

We also discussed how this move didn't make sense career-wise. Wrigley was offering a significantly bigger pay cheque. I was trading my title of 'management trainee' for 'account strategist'. There were only three other management trainees at Wrigley; Google India, on the other hand, employed hundreds of account strategists.

In hindsight, I think my parents were absolutely right! This made no logical sense. In a book titled 'How to Wreck Your Own Career Graph' this would probably rank as chapter one.

And yet …

Once we turned the corner of 'Munaf-you-are-not-making-any-sense', I was able to explain to my parents how the pay cut and loss of designation would be offset by the scale and kind of work that Google was doing globally. I had spent time doing due diligence on the role I was being offered, the company's balance sheet, its founders and Google's Silicon Valley leadership, and, of course, prospects for my own personal and professional growth within the company before I accepted their offer. Let's just say, I knew it was a sales role that entailed selling Google Ads. But I liked the idea of being a small fish in a big pond. Letting go of Wrigley was a step down but taking the role at Google was a step in the right direction for me personally.

It was the first big decision that I was making independently, one that could have long-lasting repercussions on my professional growth. My parents, though unsure about how they felt, supported and respected my choice, nonetheless.

Now here I was, four years later, seated across from Vikas not knowing what to expect. His words were still echoing.

'We've heard a lot about The Bohri Kitchen, Munaf, and we want to know what you have planned for its future.'

I felt a mixture of pride and anxiety rising within me; I was mostly terrified that I was going to lose my job for running The Bohri Kitchen on weekends while being under an employment contract with Google. I had been running this one-time-project-turned-part-time venture with my mother for eight months at the time, but I didn't ever think that it was a subject worthy of discussion with my super boss. Several thoughts were racing through my head. Was I ethically bound to disclose to my superiors at Google any details of this informal venture? Did Google own any part of my business since I developed the concept while still being employed by them?

Sensing my nervousness, Vikas quickly chimed in. 'We've heard and read a lot about what you've been up to with your mother, and I wanted to speak to you and understand if you had any serious plans to pursue it.'

Huh! Didn't see that coming.

THE BEST COMPANY
IN THE WORLD TO
WORK FOR IS THE
ONE THAT KNOWS
WHEN TO LET
YOU GO.

THE FIRST JOB GETS YOU
READY FOR THE NEXT ONE.

2

'You Have Magic in Your Hands'

My father, Turab Kapadia, toiled hard all his life. I'd like to think I get my enterprising spirit from him, and he probably gets it from my dadaji, who was also a self-made man. Originally from Rajkot in Gujarat, Dadaji moved to Mumbai (then known as Bombay) at a young age in search of better work opportunities for himself and his brothers. He was an ambitious and pragmatic man who ensured that his children—my father and his brothers and sisters—received a formal education.

Dad and his seven siblings were born and raised in Mumbai. He went from pulling a handcart at the start of his career to buying out a wholesale business from my grandfather to eventually building a plastics business that would allow his four children to pursue prestigious and meaningful careers. My three older siblings—Farzana, Aneesa and Mubbasir—are incredibly hard-working, well-qualified individuals who have placed themselves at the forefront of their respective professions.

When I got the job at Wrigley and, eventually, at Google, Dad's lifelong efforts were validated. He didn't want his children to have to expend the kind of energy he had to as an entrepreneur. For us, he wanted the comfortable, stable, 'air-conditioned' life of a corporate professional or consultant. A life that he did not have the option to pursue.

So, when I quit Google to become an entrepreneur myself, more than anything else, it shocked my father. Where did he go wrong, he wondered?

Did I make a mistake quitting Wrigley, I wondered, after I almost got fired at my first Google appraisal in September 2011. I had gone from being on the fast track to senior management with only three other guys in my cadre at Wrigley, to competing with three hundred candidates vying for a coveted, client-facing role at Google's Gurgaon (now Gurugram) and Mumbai offices, to almost being fired by Google three months into the job. How the mighty had fallen!

For me, personally, the move to Hyderabad from the hinterlands of Karnataka had been a welcome change. Back then, I looked forward to moving into a new apartment, having roommates and forging a new social circle to make up for a lifetime of being asocial. I tasted independence in small things, like buying my first bedsheet and pillow cover (Spider-Man, of course) and investing in household appliances, kitchenware and food.

Life on the Google campus was a dream. There is a reason why the company tops the employee-satisfaction charts year after year. Consider the perks—free drops and pickups, gym facilities with personal training, showers with solar-powered hot water and Biotique bath products, spa vouchers, access to the latest tech gadgets (whether for beta-testing or as Christmas gifts) and international travel to Google offices abroad. The cafeteria boasted a chaat counter, for crying out loud. And while I thoroughly enjoyed watching Lingaraju climb a coconut tree to serve us fresh nariyal paani, the all-day counter at my new job was a complete trip!

Yet ...

My first quarter in Hyderabad gave me a reality *cheque*—not just in the form of lower pay but also on where I stood in the larger scheme of things. I had upended my career from Wrigley to Google expecting to be catapulted to a position where I could fully utilize my creativity in selling the company's digital ad products. And spend the remainder of my waking hours sending emails to Larry, Sergei and Sundar about all the amazing ideas I had for them[5]!

After orientation, it dawned on me. I was one amongst hundreds of incredibly talented, hard-working and well-trained individuals who had been selected to do exactly what I was hired to do. I was no longer *the* management

---

5   Why, for God's sake, can't we set alarms within Google maps—to make the phone ring when we reach our mapped destination!

trainee, I was *an* account strategist. My job was to optimize AdWords accounts for major clients based in the US ... on behalf of their Google Account Managers (based abroad as well). At least at Wrigley, I got to sell gum to the consumer. Here, my job was to optimize the Excel sheet that would eventually be used by my foreign colleagues to sell ads to clients.

Am I complaining? Certainly not. Very early on, everyone knew that I was *that* guy who asked a lot of questions after a brief or training session. In the most chilled-out office in the country, I stayed back till 2 a.m. because, well, clearly, I had something to prove (namely, that quitting Wrigley wasn't a childish mistake). My new co-workers in Hyderabad were confident that I would ace my quarterly review.

My very first Google appraisal was a video call with my manager based in Gurgaon. I was made to realize that while the company appreciated my sense of enthusiasm and my need to submit a hundred product ideas to Google's product managers across the globe, they were dissatisfied with the quality of my work. By that, I mean *the stuff I was actually hired for*. If my ratings did not improve in the next quarter, I would be asked to resign.

As it turned out, the Excel sheets that I was sending my colleagues in Chicago were too *basic*. Clearly, I needed to focus on my core job before I could even consider doing anything else.

I wanted to continue working at Google more than ever, so the appraisal pushed me to work harder. In just the four months that I had spent there, I had already learnt a lot about systems, operations and sales. It was obvious to me that there was opportunity for professional and personal growth. So, I found myself incredible mentors within the organization to advise me on the quality of my work and to navigate the tricky rating and appraisal systems at Google. It paid off because, at the end of my third quarter, I was offered the much-lusted-after position of an 'In-Market Account Strategist' at the Mumbai office, a role that not only allowed me to directly sell ads to the Banking, Financial Services and Insurance (BFSI) sector companies across India but also consult with them on their overall digital strategy. The joy of educating the chief technology officer of State Bank of India on the potential of the internet, and to be taken seriously! The role allowed me to build castles in the air and ask others to construct them.

Through it all, the intrapreneur within me flourished. Thanks to a lot of support from my team and flexible HR policies at Google, I was also using my spare time on projects not related to my core function. These projects ranged from creating an unofficial team within the organization that volunteered time to consult with non-governmental organizatons (NGOs) on how to optimize their Google Ad Grants[6] to a forum called 'Ideafactory' which encouraged all Googlers to submit their Moonshot[7] ideas.

---

6   Google Ad Grants is a social impact programme that provides eligible non-profits around the world with up to US$10,000 per month in in-kind Google Ads.

7   A project or proposal that (a) addresses a huge problem (b) proposes a radical solution and (c) uses breakthrough technology.

Born in Hyderabad, NGO Consultants was my way of merging something I was great at (AdWords) and finding a way to convert that into social impact. Basically, we were helping NGOs make the most of the free ad credits awarded by the Google Ad Grants programme. While several NGOs had won the grant, very few were successfully using it to their benefit. Our intervention would make them eligible for even bigger grants from the company.

Ideafactory, on the other hand, was my Trojan horse. During my first few months at Google, I had realized that it's hard for a non-engineer on the lower rungs to gain the attention of senior engineers in the company. Imagine how many emails or suggestions these product managers get! I thought, if I start collating ideas from multiple Googlers, with a stamp of approval from senior leadership, then maybe someone from the L-team might actually open one of my emails and maybe, *just maybe*, one of my many ideas would bear fruit.

Working for Google gave me some of the best professional experiences of my life, but eventually, these side projects were unable to give me the dopamine fix that I desperately sought. Working a nine-to-five job as an account strategist wasn't cutting it, even if it was at the best company in the world. I was looking to satisfy an entrepreneurial itch, and this led me to pursue projects in my personal time.

That's how The Bohri Kitchen was born.

The Bohri Kitchen or TBK, as I will henceforth refer to it, was a small food venture founded by my mother and me in November 2014. The word 'Bohri' is slang for Bohra, the de rigueur classification for members of our community.

The backstory goes like this. It had been over a year since I had moved back from Hyderabad to join the Google office in Mumbai, and I was the only Kapadia kid in the house. Both my sisters had settled into lucrative careers, married and set up their own homes while my older brother had immigrated to the US. Mom's responsibilities weren't as demanding as they used to be, and she now had a lot of time on her hands. She spent it playing Candy Crush and watching saas-bahu TV shows. She was on level #2535644 of Candy Crush when things finally came to a head.

One Sunday afternoon, Mom and I fought over the TV remote. Her saas-bahu show was getting in the way of some sitcom or the other that I wanted to watch.

The back-and-forth on who would control the television set that afternoon had one positive outcome. It became clear to me that my incredibly talented mother needed something more meaningful than these OTT shows to keep her busy. So, I made it my short-term mission to find her a better alternative.

I went for the lowest hanging fruit I could find—her cooking.

I thought, if I could find a way to monetize Mom's amazing culinary talents, not only would it keep her busy and generate a small income for her, but she would thoroughly enjoy herself while doing it!

And thus began TBK, a home dining experience designed around the culinary traditions of our Dawoodi Bohra community. My grand plan to keep Mom occupied was to invite guests—people who I knew personally or through a first-degree connection—to come over to our home in Colaba and eat a meal prepared by her. I would charge them a small per head amount and give them some spiel about Bohra food.

I marketed our very first event by sending out an email featuring our elaborate lunch menu to everyone on my personal contact list. I added a line on safety measures that mentioned I'd need to speak to anyone that wanted to attend before confirming their booking. Within minutes of sending the mail, I received a flurry of responses. I was overjoyed, until I realized that almost everyone had written back asking me to stop spamming them!

The very first enquiry I received was from an extremely nice lady called Sonali. I had no idea who she was or what she did, but I was ecstatic at having received a booking. She called me up to check if we were a restaurant, which I informed her we were not, and if the event was kid-friendly—which it was! She confirmed her booking for seven people, and I was over the moon. After a couple of hours, though, I experienced a sudden rush of nerves. What if this sweet-sounding lady was a thief, or worse yet, a serial killer who now had easy access to my home and entire family?

I quickly called her back and asked her how she'd heard about us. She offered the name of a mutual friend whom I had emailed the invite to. I called this friend, who confirmed that Sonali was a very nice person, with a lovely family, and was most assuredly not a serial killer.

This gave rise to our No-Serial-Killer policy—guests cannot book a seat at TBK, they need to request one. Only after we screen guests by speaking to them, stalking them on Facebook and asking them for personal information about where they live and work, who will be accompanying them, etc., do we confirm the actual seat.

Our first event was slated for the afternoon of 20 November 2014, a Sunday. Dad had no idea what I was up to because I knew I had no chance in hell of getting him to agree to my plan of charging people to eat in our home! I simply told him I'd invited a few friends over to try Mom's food.

The meal went as planned. I welcomed our guests ever so sneakily, to ensure Dad didn't catch on. He just assumed he was talking to my friends, so whatever awkwardness hung in the air on account of being in a stranger's home on a Sunday afternoon dissipated thanks to his expert people management skills!

Highlights of the meal included the Kapadia family favourite Kaju Chicken, served with hot, wholewheat parathas, and Mom's Smoked Mutton Kheema Samosas (which eventually became TBK's signature dish). Everyone gathered around the table, excited to see what was in store for them. As people served themselves, I regaled them with chatter about every course, along with a few titbits on the Bohra community. Though reticent at first, by the time the final course of Chicken Dum Biryani came around, the guests were happy and relaxed.

It was a blissful afternoon, especially for Mom and me. The meal was a success, our guests looked pleased and we pulled if off without a hitch!

Before leaving, one of the guests walked up to Mom and hugged her. 'You have magic in your hands, aunty,' she said.

Taken aback at first, Mom lit up at this warm and genuine praise from a total stranger.

That was a defining moment for TBK. In that instance, I knew that I would first have to convince Dad to allow paying guests to eat lunch in our home.

Two successful events later, Mom and I decided to tell Dad about what we were really up to. Mom took the idea to Dad first. He wasn't thrilled. He could not imagine making customers out of guests (who normally get treated like royalty in our house). Little by little, we made him see this tiny project from my perspective. It wasn't about charging people for food, I reasoned, it was about testing whether this idea had merit. TBK would bring attention to our little community and its wonderful cuisine, which we all agreed was worthy of the spotlight.

As he had done with my switch from Wrigley to Google, Dad trusted and supported my decision even if he didn't completely agree with it. With him on board, the only thing left to do was take TBK to the kind of people up to trying a new cuisine in the home of a complete stranger!

A year later, it was clear that I had succeeded in my goal of drumming up interest for TBK, since my super boss had heard about my side hustle.

Seated across from Vikas in the Google conference room, I shared a few ideas that had crossed my mind to scale-up the business. For the first time, someone I deeply respected, a professional and my boss no less, gave me the assurance that the waves that TBK had made were worth riding. To put it in perspective, he told me that if I gave it a serious shot, one of two things would happen. Either I would fail and within a year probably find myself back at Google (or another multinational). With a five-year perspective, that wouldn't set my career back by much. On the other hand, if I succeeded, it would put my life on a completely different trajectory, one that neither he nor I could anticipate at the time.

As eager as I was to join the entrepreneurial bandwagon, quitting Google for me was never a serious option. Until now. This conversation gave me much-needed clarity, and for the first time, my business idea had been validated.

I grappled with whether quitting Google was the responsible thing to do. I had put in four years at the company and had a pretty stellar career ahead of me if I stuck with the course. I felt a sense of guilt at leaving a well-paying job to pursue what was—at this stage—only a weekend project with a lot of potential. My education and extra-curricular skills had been carefully seeded so that one day it would bear the fruit of a job at the likes of Wrigley or Google.

The most difficult part of making this decision wasn't the thought of failure, possible regret or maybe even humiliation. It was telling my parents, especially Dad. This took me back to when I decided to leave Wrigley for Google. I had a PowerPoint prepared to take Dad through the pros and cons, to prove it wasn't an impulsive, irresponsible decision.

Well, as the title of this book clearly states, I did quit Google. Most people whom I later informed about my decision reacted in one of two ways: 'Munaf, what a courageous thing to do!' or 'That sounds like a foolish decision. Who leaves a thriving career in digital advertising at Google to become a caterer?'

The truth is, neither was it a heroic decision and nor was it an irrational, impulsive one. Quitting Google to take a shot at TBK was a very well-calculated move.

Whoever said that the things that we don't do haunt us more than the things we do, was right.

3

To Eat Like a Dawoodi Bohra

When I eventually quit Google to sell samosas, I set timelines for myself, an exit strategy of sorts, that allowed me to pivot back to the employee life if I didn't achieve certain objectives within a one-year time frame. I also started working on a plan on how to take TBK to the next level.

My part-time foray into the home dining experience had been a rousing success and even Dad, who thought it unthinkable that we would charge people to eat food under our roof, started coming around.

He had laid down multiple conditions before allowing us to make the TBK Home Dining Experience official. One of them entailed memorizing fifty pages of text—basically anything and everything that he had found about the Dawoodi Bohra community—online. He made me promise that I would represent the community properly and answer questions accurately. Telling guests that the Bohra thaal was three feet in diameter because Bohras were at one point in time giants was unacceptable!

Though, if I'd been asked this question pre-TBK, that may have been my answer.

Here's a glimpse of a little that I learnt.

Dawoodi Bohras are a subsect of the Ismaili branch of Shia Islam. That sounds like a mouthful, and I could delve into the finer points of the origins and religious evolution of the Bohra community, but for the time being I'll spare us all the history lesson and distil the story of our multilayered heritage to a few fun facts.

The Bohra community was formed by splitting several times over from its Ismaili branch due to succession wars. Our religious leadership (Dai al-Mutlaq), that had built its power centre in Yemen since 1151, transferred the seat of administration of the dawat or religious mission to Sidhpur in Gujarat in 1567.

There had been a wholesome and peaceful acceptance of our unique practice of the Islamic faith across the western coast of India. Today, members of our small community are settled in large numbers across many Indian cities: Gujarat, Maharashtra, West Bengal, Rajasthan, Karnataka and Andhra Pradesh.

A consequence of migration, certain social, cultural, linguistic and economic values of the Bohra community were permanently enriched by the Gujarati communities that we came to coexist with. Bohras adopted a dialect of Gujarati as their mother tongue (what we now call 'dawat ni zubaan'); to this day, we are often mistaken for Parsis or even Gujaratis when we speak. This confusion can also be attributed to our last names. Take my own, for example—Kapadia. You'll find Gujaratis, Parsis and

Bohras with the same last name because, like the practice was at the time, we derived our last names from what we did professionally (Lokhandwala, Chitalwala, Baldiwala, Kapadia, Merchant, etc.) or where the family resided or used to reside (Pardiwala, Udaipurwala, Rajkotwala[8], etc.).

Our food was fantastically improved. From the meat-heavy diet that the dry landscape of the Middle East afforded us, we now had access to abundant green vegetables, grain, fresh fruit, dairy and whole spices that form such an important part of Indian cooking.

When I was growing up, if anyone asked me, 'Munaf, what religion do you belong to?' I would have said gaming is my religion[9]. But otherwise, any real awareness of religious identity came from Mom's food and memories of eating around a Bohra thaal—either at home on Eid, at Bohra weddings, or at the occasional religious gathering that we attended.

I do believe food gives you the easiest access into the culture of a community or family. When I first came up with the idea of calling people over and have them eat Mom's food in an attempt to keep her occupied, I was also

---

8 Fun fact—my original surname was Rajkotwala (because we are from Rajkot). But my grandfather, in his infinite wisdom, felt that one should have a surname which does not disclose one's ethnicity. Hence Kapadia. I could be Parsi, Gujarati or Bohra, you can't tell by my surname!

9 *Warcraft, Tomb Raider, Diablo, Populous, Age of Empires, Baldur's Gate* ... oh my God, this book should have been called 'How I Quit Gaming to Sell Samosas'.

simultaneously thinking *how exciting would it be for a non-Bohra to eat around a thaal?*

For those of you who have never had the chance to eat from a thaal, let me paint a picture of what a typical meal around a thaal looks like.

According to tradition, us Bohras sit on the floor on a square cloth mat called a safra and eat from a thaal, which is a large steel platter. The average thaal is three feet in diameter and placed on top of a kundli (anything that gives the thaal a slight elevation). Seven or eight hungry guests can be seated around it, cross-legged (or somewhere between cross-legged and a padmasana[10]) so that everyone can reach the centre of the thaal. At any Bohra function, you are likely to find yourself randomly sitting around a thaal, shoulder-to-shoulder with complete strangers.

At the end of the meal, you will either hate your fellow diners because somebody grabbed your samosa before you could get to it. Or, in all likelihood, you will make friends, get the latest on the chawl gossip and maybe even crack a potential business partnership!

At the TBK Home Dining Experience, while we wait for all the diners to arrive, we serve our signature Nariyal Paani Cooler—tender coconut or malai blended with sweet coconut water. According to Bohra custom, guests are first offered something sweet (not water) as a gesture of hospitality. We found a middle ground to satisfy our guests, many of whom arrive parched after having climbed

---

10 When I wrote this chapter, I had just finished two months of yoga. It's awesome, you should try it!

two flights of stairs. We hand out name tags to guests; in a roomful of strangers that you will be intimately dining with, this helps break the ice.

Once all the guests arrive and have been seated[11], a pre-plated thaal is placed before them on a low coffee-table with condiments and a neemak daani. At my house, condiments served include Pudina Chutney, Pineapple and Boondi Raita, Aam Chunda (a sweet raw mango preserve with chilli powder), Kokam Aloo (potatoes cooked in a tart kokam masala), Bhavnagari Mirchis, Aamba Halad (two types of fresh turmeric and black pepper pickled in vinegar) and a bowl of lemon wedges. Yes, these are just the condiments! They may vary depending on seasonality.

The neemak daani is a small dish containing salt. Traditionally, before the meal can begin, any one enthusiastic participant seeking good karma will volunteer to pick up the neemak daani with both hands and offer salt to the others seated around the thaal. We offer a quick prayer as we take a pinch of salt to cleanse our palate and activate our salivary glands for what is going to be a fantastic meal. Sometimes we encourage (read: *bully*) the youngest member on the thaal to *volunteer*!

I'm not surprised the average non-Bohra is flummoxed by this ritual (we've had guests throw salt above their heads). I've seen people eye the steel thaal clearly wondering if it's an individual plate for each of them!

---

11 At the TBK Home Dining Experience, guests have the option of sitting on chairs with the thaal placed on a table. Cramps can be a very real thing for those of non-Bohra origin.

Our concept of eating from a thaal has its roots in our origins in the Middle East. Eating from a large shared plate had manifold benefits for the nomadic Arabs. With several people flanking a thaal, I imagine it reduces the chances of any sand or desert wind blowing into your food. In countries where water is scarce, having to clean and wash one big utensil as opposed to several smaller utensils could've also been the practical reason why eating from a single thaal was common. Food wastage reduces significantly as well. Lastly, there is a certain bonding theme at play here. Like in most communities, sharing at least one meal together as a family is sacrosanct. Sharing a meal with outsiders is a show of inclusion and bonhomie. If someone studied this further, and I am certain someone has, dining concepts and mealtimes must have helped maintain power structures at a tribal level.

At TBK, while we explain the significance of the thaal, we also tell our guests how to eat from it. Comparing it to sharing a pizza, we explain their section of the thaal is the 'slice' that is closest to them. Typically, diners are expected to clean up the thaal (a sign of having enjoyed the meal and an indicator of the discipline with which the diner has eaten, never taking more than required[12]). Bohras know

---

12 Telling paid customers to make sure they don't waste anything can easily be misconstrued. So I tell our guests that 'At the end of the meal, the thaal should be filled with so much colour from all the chutneys and masalas that you literally won't be able to see anything! But there should be no food left over.'

better than to leave a stray grain of rice or remnants of any chutney or pickle in their corner.

The food is served on a thaal course-wise, starting with a kharaas or savoury item such as our now-famous Smoked Mutton Kheema Samosas. This may be followed by a Nariyal Kebab (tiny vegetarian kebabs stuffed with mashed potato, spring onions and desiccated coconut). Over the years, when we've had too much ruckus once the meal begins, I've taken help from a steel plate and spoon to get everyone's attention. And just like Pavlov, I condition my guests to associate the sound of a steel spoon hitting the plate with the onset of the next course!

The kharaas is followed by a meethas or a sweet dish. (Alternating between savoury and sweet is a tradition we follow; it helps balance the gut and allows you to indulge in seven courses of food.) An example of a classic Bohra meethas is the outstanding Malai Khaja[13], a kind of Bohra Baklava.

Once you've reset your palate and activated those digestive juices, we move onto more serious food such as the Legendary Raan in Red Masala[14]which is a one kilo-plus leg of a goat marinated for over two days and cooked on a high-pressure flame for a couple of hours. Served on the bone, it is garnished with salli wafer and coriander. Ogling guests usually wait patiently for someone to debone and

---

13 A whole pastry dipped in sugar syrup stuffed with fresh malai.

14 What do you call it when everyone goes a little silent, almost in a food coma, after eating the raan? Silence of the Lambs.

serve it. Obviously, we don't do that; instead, we explain that the real test of a well-prepared raan is whether it's tender enough for you to use your hands to pull the meat off the bone. At this point, guests let go of their inhibitions and the name tags come in handy. When a 'Rohan' is asking 'Dr Pradeep' to hold on to the plate while he serves himself, that's called 'breaking bread at TBK'.

The next course is the jaman aka main course—it could be Kaari Chawal (curry made from ground peanuts, coconut milk, dry fruits and whole spices) or a Bohra Dum Biryani (multiple layers of rice, masala, marinated vegetables/meat and the signature potatoes). Most meat lovers are scornful when we tell them that we add potatoes, but they are usually the ones to ask for second helpings of these flavour bombs.

By the jaman course, there's usually a dramatic turnaround in the atmosphere in the room[15]. The cheerful, loud and energetic group of diners now appear half-asleep, barely able to get up to return the crockery and cutlery to the staff. When they hear that the meal is not over, they react with disbelief.

Next up is Sancha Ice Cream. A 'saancha' is a big wooden barrel with a steel cylinder fitted inside. Between the inner wall of the barrel and the cylinder there's a lot

---

15 Along with the Biryani, at TBK, we always serve what we call an emergency beverage—the Jal Jeera Soda—that you will either love or hate, but we urge you to chug down a glass for the benefits you will reap a few hours later.

of ice. The cylinder itself is filled with milk, fresh fruit and absolutely no emulsifiers or stabilizers. The ice cream, either fresh sitaphal (custard apple) or peru (guava) with red chilli powder, is hand churned and served.

The ice cream is followed by some amazing Gundi Paan—sourced from Dad's neighbourhood paanwala—bringing an end to this gastronomic journey.

Minus the mouth-watering food, I've pretty much summed up the TBK Home Dining Experience. We don't eat with our guests, but spend a lot of time taking them through every course, saying funny things that no one laughs at[16] and basically ensuring that when someone is done with the meal and leaves our home, they do so not only with full stomachs, but full hearts and minds as well. They leave knowing what a Bohra family is, what we believe in and represent, and a little more sensitized to the different cultures that exist around us.

If my MBA in marketing and four years at Google taught me anything, it's that the world's best brands and businesses are built on authenticity, creativity and their ability to give customers something unique.

Now, imagine if you knew nothing about our culture or eating practices, and you were taken through the whole

---

16 Now that you know what kharaas-meethas is, I can tell you a famous Bohra phrase Dad always recites to guests: 'Bey (two) kharaas, bey meethas, ek (one) bypass, Bohra khalaas (is dead).'

experience of eating home-made Bohra fare in the home of a Bohra family as their guests. Wouldn't that be an experience worth hosting every weekend?

The entrepreneur in me had recognized there was a business opportunity in my culinary heritage. Every thaal I ate from had triggered the same thought—why is this not available commercially outside the community?

I gave it some more thought and did what I do when I have rocket-science-level-problems to solve. I created a Google spreadsheet—and I made a formula.

23 May 2019: Facebook Live of me hosting a Home Dining Experience

CREATING THAT FIRST SOCIAL MEDIA PAGE IS AS IMPORTANT AS RAISING A MILLION BUCKS.

EVERY SMALL VICTORY LEADS TO THE BIG ONES.

4

The Recipe for a Sumptuous Brand

Before the very first time we threw our Colaba home open to guests as TBK in November 2014, even before I sent out the menus for our first event, I had conceptualized TBK's logo.

For as long as I can remember, I have fantasized about taking Bohra food to a non-Bohra audience. After I had found the perfect reason to finally do it—put Mom's prolific culinary talent to use—I could hardly wait to create that powerhouse brand.

The name—The Bohri Kitchen—came to me first. It was simple, straightforward and urban. A lot of restaurants and cafés were using the word 'kitchen' in their branding. I was also aware that not a lot of people would be familiar with the word Bohri. For a layperson, it might not represent or suggest Islamic or Middle Eastern roots, so I thought I'd use evocative typography to convey that. I Googled 'Muslim font' and was pleasantly surprised to find a match within minutes of browsing. The font was called Pseudo Saudi[17] and I typed out T-h-e B-o-h-r-i K-i-t-c-h-e-n in that font. I was delighted with the results!

the bohri kitchen™

the bohri kitchen

I also created an acronym using the same Pseudo Saudi font; today it is our more commonly used logo.

If you've created branded content for your own company or someone else's, you'll be familiar with that deep sense of satisfaction that comes from nailing a concept that only existed in your mind. It makes your idea real, tangible almost. This was that moment for me.

I gave the brand a bipolar personality disorder (my personality—narcissistic, my parents' personality—warm) and multiple product associations that weren't necessarily even from the same industry (home dining, catering, delivery and someday even a book!). I needed flexibility in branding (because there was so much more I wanted to do) and so the logo I visualized was a single font in monochromatic tones.

---

17 And in this manner, I created a Pseudo Logo! I mean, at that time I was certain that this would be a temporary logo. Who creates a logo for a company valued at ₹10 crore using a public font available on the internet? Well, apparently, I do! We're still very much using the same logo.

I haven't changed the logo in five years and have used it on merchandise, packaging, social media pages, our website, business cards, invites and the like.

You're probably wondering how I got away with pulling this cheap designing trick. People do, after all, spend thousands, even lakhs, of rupees to create branding—but I didn't. I hadn't even procured a licence for commercial use from the creator of the font. It was only after we received some press coverage that I went back to the source website for the font and read the fine print on its commercial use. It confirmed what I already knew—the font was not *freely* available! I wondered how much I owed the font creator for it.

As I have on many other occasions running TBK, I somehow caught a lucky break. After a quick search, I managed to find the font artist who offered the logo for infinite commercial use after a donation of US$20. I made the payment on the spot and voila! the font was mine to use commercially forever.

This was a big victory for me personally. For me, the limited visual branding I had created for TBK was everything. We have been gifted artwork with TBK hand-drawn and even stitched on surfaces by loyal customers. I was so deeply attached to the logo that I was almost willing to shut the business down if I didn't get the license to commercially use the logo!

With the logo ready in record time, I could spend more time to create the actual invite and menu that I needed to send out.

We would get enquiries or bookings based on that email, so I spent a considerable amount of time on it. Wary of dull writing, a misplaced comma or spelling errors, I pored over the copy for hours. I paid careful attention to every detail— such as the beverages and condiments we paired with the food. I have come to realize that it's the small details that make the customer take you seriously. It's not just about a gorgeous leg of lamb in our legendary red masala, it's also about describing the salli wafers that go on top that give it that little crunch and break the monotony of red masala with golden flecks of fine crisp potato chips.

Next, to make sure that guests came to the experience mentally prepared to do justice to seven courses, we decided to create a WhatsApp group a day prior to the event and share critical information with them. The importance of being punctual (so that we could begin and end the meal in a timely fashion) and the fact that our eighty-year-old building didn't have a lift (guests would have to climb two flights of stairs to reach our apartment) were mentioned.

Most marketing professionals will tell you that in today's saturated marketplace, the key to visibility and staying top of mind is creating content. After the first TBK Home Dining Experience went off without a hitch, I created Facebook and Instagram pages to share menus, photos of the food we served, communication around upcoming events, etc. The brand needed to be positioned in a certain way so that it appealed to the right clientele who, in turn, would help promote and mould the brand into what I envisioned for it.

When we started in November 2014, we barely managed to achieve the minimum bookings that I needed to justify an event on most weekends. It was only after the few initial experiences and by bribing[18] our guests to leave a review or check-in on social media that word about us started to get around.

We began by charging ₹700 per seat and continued with the same rate for a few months. But as our menu grew, so did our popularity, and we took the liberty to raise the price per seat. This proved challenging, in part because of the misassumptions people have about home dining. For instance, in our case, it was Mom—whom the average person will refer to as 'aunty'—cooking the food. A home chef isn't considered on par with a professional chef. People were willing to pay to eat her food, just not as much as the food was worth because we weren't operating out of a commercial establishment and our overheads were minimal. The latter may have been true, but we also had to keep the numbers low, and the clientele as selective as possible, as we were inviting guests into our home.

---

18 I would shamelessly offer our guests a baby jar of Mom's phenomenal khajur chutney in exchange for a testimonial on social media (good or bad, of course). It helped that the average rating we got was 4.9 out of 5.

To combat this misconception and what I called 'aunty business', I put in extra effort to make our marketing and communication as credible and authentic as possible. We shared photographs[19] that looked like they're out of a *MasterChef Australia* episode even as we leveraged the sincere sentiments associated with 'maa ke haath ka khaana'. In our communication, we never tried to compete with professional chefs and the amazing work they do, but instead established food made by Nafisa Kapadia as something unparalleled. I saw Mom's rustic skills, her 'cooking with andaaz', as an asset and not a liability. Instead of apologizing for our lack of seating space, air conditioning, lift or even parking, I charged a premium for it. This uncompromising, unapologetic approach towards brand TBK and our food is what finally earned us comparisons with some of the best food and beverage (F&B) experiences in the world.

It also made it easier for me to sell out at what later became our base price point—₹1,500. By capping bookings even in circumstances where I could have taken more clients, I created opportunities to tell my fan base that we're sold out. Nothing generates more demand than a perceived lack of supply.

My marketing professors would be proud to watch how I played with pricing and the illusion of scarcity. By early

---

19 As with all great things that happened with TBK, our first portfolio of professional shots was thanks to an amazing photographer duo Shefali and Anisha Lanewala, who call themselves Chaiwallahs and did this for us at a huge discount.

2015, I had started collaborating with big brands and did niche, highly priced TBK Home Dining Experiences aka 'The Mother of all Feasts' (₹3,500-6,000 per seat). These collaborations gave me access to the databases and heavy-duty marketing arsenal that these big brands possessed, which helped sell out of these events.

Our message was: no matter how many Bohra cuisine restaurants crop up in the future or Bohra weddings you attend, eating food prepared by Nafisa Kapadia from a thaal at the Kapadia home is always going to be a different experience.

5

Before the Thaal, There Was The Dining Table

I'm very sorry to say this but the title of this book is a lie—I never quit Google to sell samosas.

I quit to create the Airbnb of home dining experiences!

The what?

I'll explain.

By April 2015, while I was still at Google, TBK went viral (more on that later). I was inundated with messages on Facebook and Instagram as well as emails from home chefs (amateur cooks operating food businesses from home).

Inspired and motivated by 'Nafisa aunty's' success, they'd ask me for advice on how to generate sales and gain visibility for their products and services.

Never one to miss an opportunity to evangelize, I wrote back to several home chefs offering brief suggestions on what they could do. I even met some of them personally to see if I could add value to their brands.

Our streak of home dining experiences was going strong[20]. Operations were now fully managed by my parents; my role was limited to creating the TBK Facebook page. We had stepped up our game and with Monu and Anjum—our incredible helpers at home—created a standard operating procedure (SOP) covering service, ambience and decor, duration, payment, guest interactions, etc. For three hours at lunchtime, on many weekends since November 2014, our Colaba living room was transformed into a lavish fete.

The momentum in business gave me the necessary push to start working on a business plan. While I realized that I had a shot at capitalizing on my food heritage, it never occurred to me that TBK itself could become a multi-vertical F&B business. I mean, come on. Creating a start-up selling Bohra food? Barely anyone knew anything about the community. Most of my friends thought I was Parsi! Also, I knew absolutely nothing about the F&B industry. On the other hand, tech disruption, uberization, creating platforms ... this was right up my sleeve. Working at Google for three-plus years had planted crazy, ambitious ideas in my head. It made me live, breathe and sometimes even eat 10x[21]. Ultimately, instead of selling samosas, the

---

20 Since we started TBK in November 2014, we always—without a doubt—made a profit. We did not chase sales, we chased value.

21 Google slang for growing something ten times beyond its current reach.

idea of creating a 'guaranteed billion-dollar start-up' idea seemed far more exciting.

And so, the Airbnb of home dining experiences was born!

I started putting my thoughts down on a PowerPoint presentation. I was driven by two key thoughts. One, while the supply of regional cuisines in India is staggering, most of these cuisines are either not represented or under-represented in India's F&B sector. Two, the underutilized Indian housewife. Most of the home chefs who approached me for collaborations, advice and marketing assistance had been women. More specifically, housewives who were raising families, not pursuing careers. The responsibility of running a home can be a hard and thankless[22] task, and my objective was to create a window of opportunity where enterprising women like Mom could monetize their culinary skills and promote their culture without having to step too far out of their comfort zone.

And so, even before I quit Google, my goal was to scale home dining experiences as a concept using a tech platform and focused digital marketing.

---

22 In my home, every time Mom would serve us lunch, instead of acknowledging it and being thankful for how great the meal was, our standard response would be, 'Mom, what's for dinner?' The shock on Mom's face when a guest once hugged her at the end of a meal clearly showed how she was totally unaccustomed to this type of appreciation.

Most of the home chefs who had written in asked me questions about brand building, public relations (PR) and sales. Instead of writing back to each one of them with suggestions, I came up with a better solution.

I decided to get the home chefs under the same roof (mine) with a potluck. My only condition was that everyone who attended needed to bring a dish prepared by them.

And boy, what a turnout we had! From bakers and fromagers to keto specialists, some twenty-plus home chefs landed up, filling every square inch of my ten-seater dining table with quiche, lasagne, Karela Biryani, Kung Pao Potatoes, Feta Cheese Salad, raan and Nariyal Kebab (Mom's contribution), burritos, nachos with an assortment of dips, freshly-baked brownies, a decadent apple pie, carrot cake, Bhapa Doi, etc. Over a wonderful meal, each home chef spoke briefly about their respective businesses. Before the lunch ended, we decided to keep in touch, meet more often and bring new home chefs into the fold.

A WhatsApp group, which I christened 'Home Chef Revolution', was created. The objective of this group was to provide a forum for the home chef community to discuss their challenges, ask questions, share solutions and help members network by sharing personal connections.

There was a wonderful bonhomie that formed among the members of this group and the information exchange proved to be a great learning for me as well. It only reinforced my belief that there was a business opportunity here. These micro-entrepreneurs were remarkable at what they did, and I was convinced that my plan for them was sound.

By the time I quit Google in July 2015, the Home Chef Revolution community had grown by leaps and bounds. I volunteered to hold sessions on marketing and branding at people's homes, using this opportunity to accumulate a database of names, educational profile, culinary specializations and other information. I also rated their interest levels (i.e., how keen they were to build their business). All of this was done keeping the Airbnb of home dining experiences at the back of my mind. With every new home chef I met, my conviction grew stronger.

This is how it would work—much like Airbnb, Uber and Zomato aggregate homestays, cabs and restaurants respectively, a tech solution to the home chef dilemma of 'how do I get seen on the internet?' would collect experiences/services offered by home chefs that customers could avail of in a few simple steps. It would enable home chefs to create events, share their stories, photos, cultural context, provide a booking page and payment gateway through which customers could purchase tickets and items in real time. In turn, customers would be able to review experiences and rate them, provide direct feedback and bookmark/save experiences for later. You would also be able to follow individual home chefs and track their presence at pop-ups and flea markets. I wanted to create a small industry, on the back of this one idea.

I had in-depth discussions about my idea with the Home Chef Revolution group and was reassured to know that they saw value in my proposed platform.

Next, I started on the app through which consumers would interact with these chefs. I decided we would need an interface that could support beautiful photographs along with powerful personal stories and sparkling writing to draw in potential guests. The goal was to ensure seats were always sold out; to make people request a seat and NOT book one.

A month later, I came up with the name 'The Dining Table' (TDT) for the app. My marketing brain wanted a name or phrase that represented something that most home dining experiences would have in common and that could easily fit into call for actions like—'Come join us at The Dining Table', 'This week on The Dining Table' or 'What's on The Dining Table?'... you get the drift.

It was a huge milestone for me. Besides, constantly referring to the idea as the Airbnb of home dining experiences was taxing and giving Airbnb free publicity!

To design the user interface, I sought help from Samudra Gupta, an ex-Googler. I referenced an app from China and even hired a Mandarin translator to help me understand the workings of the Chinese app better. Then I made my own interface.

*The TDT logo! In case you're a doofus and don't get it—the T is a table,
H are chairs. BOOM!*

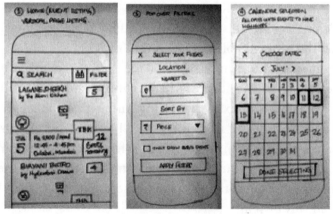

UI drawings made with Samudra's help.

A friend of mine, who is a serial entrepreneur himself, once told me that the one mistake some of the best entrepreneurs make—when starting out—is that they forget to Google whether someone is already pursuing the great idea they came up with. They either forget or do it too late, usually because they don't want to hear someone else has beaten them to the finish line!

In my opinion, it's actually a great thing if someone else has already worked on your idea. There is absolutely no better way to start on a business idea than to study and learn from other peoples' successes—or even better—failures!

A little, but not too late[23] in the development of TDT, I found myself Googling 'home dining experiences' and found that multiple people across the globe had attempted to create the Airbnb of home dining experiences but absolutely nobody had succeeded. Many of these entrepreneurs had managed to raise millions in the first round of funding, but no one had been able to secure a second round (a good indicator that the idea had not clicked). In fact, at home in India as well, there was a great attempt by Meal Tango to do the exact same thing. They had failed to scale their business and, at the time this book was written, they had pivoted to delivery.

I studied these business models meticulously, reading interviews by investors and founders, trying to see if there was anything I could do differently.

---

23 Maybe the book should have been titled 'The Guy who Quit Google to pursue an Idea that he forgot to Google'.

My research showed me that the space was already heating up internationally, with home dining aggregators called Cookening (France), Feastly (US) and EatWith (Israel). But by far, the hottest one was VizEat, a European venture which eventually raised a whopping €3.8 million in 2016 and claimed to have 20,000 hosts across 110 countries!

Yet, none of these guys had successful exits as of February 2020—at least none that were headline-worthy.

At this stage, I pushed myself to do something I had been dreading for some time—market research. I wanted to test my assumption that there's a market for home dining experiences in India. I was so focused on the supply side that, for a moment, I hadn't given too much thought to the demand side. I guess I just assumed that since TBK was doing phenomenally well (we were selling out weeks in advance), why wouldn't other home dining experiences on my platform experience the same celebrity?

I made a list of fifty friends and family, choosing people from different age groups and income levels, and living across Mumbai. I pitched the app to everyone I called, explaining in great detail how it would work, the benefit to home chefs, the kind of home dining experiences users would be able to choose from and the price points of such experiences. I asked them, 'Would you buy a seat at The Dining Table?'

Almost everyone said, *NO*.

I had quit Google for this idea, invested months and over ₹1 lakh in it, roused the enthusiasm of a bunch of home chefs and convinced my parents that I was onto something big. I even convinced investors to commit ₹35 lakh towards the project. Now, suddenly, I was completely unsure about whether this would work.

I asked all the respondents, a bit defensively, 'You've come to TBK multiple times, why would you not want to try a home dining experience by another home chef?' Their answer was simple. To them, TBK is a brand with tremendous credibility. This took away their concerns about eating in an unknown person's home. One of the respondents even said, 'How do you tell an aunty that you didn't like the food and want a refund?' Booking in advance, high price points and having to travel long distances to the home chefs' homes were other barriers.

It was becoming evident that creating the Airbnb of home dining experiences would not be an easy task. It was *definitely* not something that could be done with ₹35 lakh; it required an extremely talented team, a couple of million dollars in funding (or a strong partner who already has a powerful captive market) and a guerrilla marketing crew on the lines of what Netflix today has. I was attempting to create a parallel F&B industry which would operate in tandem with restaurants, quick service restaurants (QSRs) and delivery chains.

I was onto something as disruptive as Airbnb or Uber, and hence this would require the kind of muscle that these players have. I would have to wait for the right opportunity to reattempt The Dining Table.

It then occurred to me that, perhaps, the opportunity to scale-up was right under my nose. Taking TBK to the next level and exploring its full potential might put me in a better position to create TDT someday.

On that thought, I pressed pause on the TDT app and decided to focus on building my home-grown business instead.

Hungry for more detail? Here's the presentation I had made to a venture capitalist fund in July 2015 on The Dining Table that earned me ₹35 lakh worth of investment interest.

THE BIGGEST MISTAKE ENTREPRENEURS MAKE IS THEY FORGET TO GOOGLE THEIR IDEA.

SECOND BIGGEST MISTAKE? NOT REALIZING YOU CAN LEARN FROM WHAT OTHERS DID WRONG.

6

The Weekend That Almost Ended TBK

Seated with my laptop, and feeding people every weekend in my living room, I had managed to create a successful home-grown business while working full time at Google. Back then, I didn't feel motivated to take TBK outside our Colaba home. I don't know if this was arrogance on my part or nervousness at being pitted against other F&B ventures. The thought of going from an invite-only kind of brand to a food start-up trying to hard sell itself gave me the jitters. The Mumbai food scene is competitive and brimming with talent. Besides, I was focused on developing the TDT app at the time and was content with maintaining status quo with TBK—weekend meals at home only.

That changed in May 2015, a month before I quit my job. I had met Insia Lacewalla and Paresh Chhabria, the duo that ran the Small Fry Company, through the Home Chef Revolution. Small Fry brought together small and exciting food and lifestyle brands through curated pop-ups and festivals. I was genuinely impressed by the duo as well, which encouraged me to consider a collaboration despite my reservations about taking TBK out of the house.

The Bombay Local was one of the events organized by the Small Fry Company, a one-evening affair of a collection of small home-grown ventures like ours. Mom seemed quite confident about pulling this stint off. We put together a small, easy-to-execute menu. Sixty-five plates of Kaju Chicken and Jeera Rice, thirty plates of Biryani and four hundred Smoked Mutton Kheema Samosas. This was the first time Mom had used our one hundred square feet kitchen at home to prepare quantities of food large enough to feed over a hundred people. In the twenty-four hours before the event, every square inch of the kitchen was being used to chop, marinate, heat, pack or store the food. Despite the chaos and the mess, Mom looked genuinely happy—and a little tired—at the challenge of feeding so many people.

I didn't want to invest heavily in any marketing collaterals. (I figured our appearance at pop-ups would be a one-off, so why spend?) Patiently, I printed out individual lettering in Pseudo Saudi font to create a sign that said 'The Bohri Kitchen'. I had A4 sheets laminated by a xeroxwala whose shop was just below our flat. Then I painstakingly punched holes into each laminated printout and found a ribbon to string it up. Proud of my jugaad, I decided to put the sign together at the event. Little did I realize that a few letters would be hard to tell apart, because of which I had to arrange and rearrange the letters a few times to get the order right!

The DIY signage was the only thing that proved to be a complication that evening. The event was set to begin at 4 p.m.; the first wave of hungry festival-goers came in at around 6 p.m. and for the next hour, we didn't have a second to ourselves. By 7.15 p.m. we were sold out!

At home, our dining experiences are curated, slow-paced and intimate. Here, orders were coming at us from all directions and we had just a small table barricading us against the crowds. You'd imagine that the people lining up, drinks in hand, shouting their orders over music blaring from large speakers would be overwhelming. But really, it was exhilarating.

The crowd at the event—young, urban—was exactly the demographic that I was hoping would experiment and engage with a brand like mine. Many people who had been home to eat, or had read about us, bought food from our stall that evening; a few people dropped by just to say hello. After the response we received, Mom and I looked forward to more such events and collaborations.

The Bombay Local experience was a milestone, both for me personally[24] and for TBK. After quitting my Google job, I had become obsessed with the need to scale TBK. The

---

24 This food festival was special for another reason as well — my wife (and co-author of this book!), Zahabia, was also present, eating away to glory with her friends. To think, we never met each other until almost two years later. To think, she could have met the love of her life (aka me) sooner.

Dining Table app did not take off like I had expected but I began to see how TBK most certainly could if we did more to put ourselves out there. I started speaking with other home chefs on the Home Chef Revolution chat group and we set up our first-ever pop-up at a five-star hotel soon after. Mom and I even did our first out-of-city pop-up in Chennai! I began speaking to restaurateurs, retailers and chefs to evaluate the feasibility of opening a restaurant and selling our signature samosas and chutneys at stores.

Meanwhile, the home dining experiences continued with full steam. I also dabbled in delivery with Trekurious and Hola Chef. While this delivery service meant pre-orders of food from a limited menu that Mom could prepare comfortably from home, it did plant the seeds of TBK on-demand delivery. But more on that later.

By December 2015, I snagged TBK the opportunity to participate in a massive music festival at Pune. Apart from the obvious lure of participating in a music festival (the energy, the crowd, the cool quotient), I was using this opportunity to test an idea I had been toying with for a long time.

With some trepidation, I took the plunge and decided to outsource production of the food to an experienced chef and his team. I had already identified someone who would be fit for the job. Mom had her hands full with TBK's Home Dining Experiences and spending hours standing in a food stall at a music fest was not something she wanted to do. This was a good chance to see whether I could replicate Mom's success without her being personally involved.

I had planned a fun, booze-friendly menu. We were going to do Khatta Meetha Chicken Drumsticks with French Fries, Smoked Mutton Kheema Samosas (packaged popcorn-style), Chicken Russian Cutlets (a bestseller) and Chana Bateta Thulli[25] for vegetarians.

I asked Mom to note down the exact recipes[26] for the menu we had planned. Then, I put together a team of kitchen helpers to help us prepare the food and manage the stall. Lastly, I made plans to crash with my friend Vivek Vishwekar, whom I had met on a Himalayan cycling expedition three years earlier, in Pune.

As I embarked on this new adventure, memories of this mountain biking expedition organized by the Youth Hostel Association of India came back to me. My friend and Google colleague at the time, Gaurav Shinde, had convinced me to join this crazy adventure. It was a seven-day excursion, cycling up and down Jalori Pass at the base of the Himalayas, roughly ten thousand kilometres above sea level.

---

25 A niche Bohra speciality made with kala chana, small potatoes and a mild masala, eaten as a snack.

26 Mom simply doesn't know how to note down recipes. If you ask her how much red chilli powder goes into her Biryani masala for a kilo of Biryani, she'll make a small fist with her hand. This might also be the magic behind our recipes, how she makes it with 'andaaz'—but this was also the reason why, in my attempts at standardizing and scaling our food, most of my hair has turned white today.

Only, I didn't how to cycle. As a child, I had developed an irrational fear of falling off a bike and hurting myself. Being unable to ride had always been a source of shame for me. Participating in this cycling trip was my way of pushing myself to just get over it; I thought it would unlock a world of adventures. And it worked!

Over those seven days, as we cycled from base to base, I would always be the last one to enter camp. By the time I'd get off my bike, the others had already cooled down, cleaned up and started a game of cards. But not once did I feel or was made to feel embarrassed. For me, it was enough knowing that whatever happened, how many ever times I fell of that bike, or thought I was going to pass out from fatigue (and even that one time when I actually got lost!), whatever the circumstances, I knew I was going to finish what I had started.

I think taking that stall at the Pune festival was a similar attempt to overcome another unspoken fear lurking at the back of my mind—*had I made a mistake quitting Google?* I had to make a go of it.

When we departed from Mumbai, on the first day of the festival, I felt positive and excited viewing the entire experience as an adventure rather than a job. After travelling for about three hours in a tempo, we reached the little dhaba that was supposed to be the production centre for the event.

The plan was to prepare the food in a kitchen not too far from the venue and transport it daily for the three-day festival. On reaching the site, however, we realized that our dhaba kitchen was at a four hours' distance from the venue of the event. We would have to make two trips a day, over three days, to transport all the food.

How could I have let this happen?

I immediately began looking for an alternate place to prepare our food. At the same time, we needed to pull this gig off with the existing set-up for day one of the festival. The event opened for ticket holders in the evening, and we had only a few hours to rush to the venue, set up our stall and fire things up. Or should I say, fry things up!

To curb my growing sense of panic as I watched the team scramble, I went over all the opportunities this event presented—a new target audience (hopefully, groupies who would develop a samosa addiction and follow TBK wherever we went), investors in Pune ... I might even charm a girl with my newly grown and groomed moustache! Moreover, being in a new city with our food at a much-anticipated music festival was a high that I wasn't ready to come down from just yet.

We reached the venue in the nick of time; I saw that the other food stalls were almost set up and ready for business.

That's when I received a second jolt. The food court was located far away from the performance areas. There was palpable tension in the air as stall owners and helpers discussed how this could significantly impact footfalls in the F&B section.

On that first evening, as the show went on, the food court saw a thin crowd. Unfortunately for us, the TBK stall was practically empty compared to the others. My initial concerns about us running out of food seemed unfounded now. Our sales were dismal. As difficult as it is for me to admit, the quality of the food might also have had something to do with it. My gamble of outsourcing production didn't pay off. To my chagrin, my formulaic approach to cooking—noting down recipes, organizing ingredients, handing it all over to a chef and expecting Mom's quality of food—had not worked. At this time, my respect for Mom's technique and cooking style had tripled. I missed her thoroughly.

The next two days of the event passed in much the same way. We were approached by a lot of familiar faces—people from Mumbai who had been home or had heard about us. I was deeply embarrassed that these people, who had seen the brand at its best, were now witness to its seemingly worst moment.

Even if we didn't sell out, I didn't want to think that our food not being up to the mark was the cause of it.

My helpers at the stall were low on morale as well. I had promised them incentives based on sales, but it was clear that all they would be making was base pay. I was so jittery about the back-of-the-house mood that I refused to leave the counter even for a second, fearing that the boys would make a run for it the second I turned my back.

By day three, I accepted that this event was going to be a dud for TBK. Sales were abysmal and my spirits had deep dived into a pool of unsold khatta meetha sauce (aka pity and self-doubt). I felt silly for not having planned better, for lacking the operational know-how to reasonably anticipate production-related hiccups, and for having agreed to do this without Mom's input entirely. I desperately felt the need for a co-founder, someone who could manage operational and production challenges the way I could tackle the marketing and branding ones.

Ideally, Mom was supposed to be that person, but she enjoyed managing our home dining experiences. She felt that played to her strengths—working from her own kitchen and home, where she could curate experiences and control the quality and scale of the food to the best of her abilities. However, if the brand had to reach a wider audience, go from niche to mainstream, from a part-time project to a full-blown F&B business that could be scaled, it needed to adapt to other models as well—catering, delivery, pop-ups, food stalls, etc. I felt a bit lost and overwhelmed as these big questions loomed large.

Before 2015 ended, I needed to give TBK some kind of direction. I needed the business to generate an income for me, one that was substantial enough to justify leaving the best company in the world and to show Dad that quitting Google to sell samosas wasn't as ludicrous as it sounded.

7

Do You Deliver?

L ooking back, I may have exaggerated just how big a setback the Pune event was. It's taken me five years to come to terms with the fact that the food business is tenuous, especially when you're starting out and don't have proper systems in place.

Back in Mumbai, I began to work on a broader plan to diversify TBK into a food delivery business. Why home delivery, you ask, given that the ideal setting for a thaal experience and slow-cooked Bohra food would be a restaurant?

You're absolutely right. A restaurant would be the natural progression for TBK's Home Dining Experience. It's every home chef's dream. It's what we, as a family, collectively fantasized about when TBK started gaining popularity. There were two things holding us back, however. One was the intensive capital requirement to set up and operate a restaurant. Second was the fact that neither Mom nor I had commercial hospitality experience.

In the first six months after quitting Google, I had spoken to several home chefs and restaurant operators, all of whom highlighted the various risks associated with setting up a restaurant in a city like Mumbai. That further cemented my decision to take a different route to expand TBK.

Food delivery looked promising from both an investment and branding point of view. I come from the tech industry, where the go-to business model is generating revenue using minimal, tangible assets and a wealth of digital products. I wanted to adopt a similar approach and decided to pursue an on-demand, food delivery-business model for TBK. At the time, Zomato, Swiggy, Scootsy and a score of other logistics platforms had appeared on the Indian F&B scene, making food delivery for restaurant and small food-business operators increasingly viable. I would only need a dark kitchen (or what is now referred to as a cloud kitchen) to prepare and send out food on demand to hungry customers through one of our logistics partners.

During the food delivery ideation phase, I had also given careful thought to how I would optimize the TBK menu for delivery. Bohra food is considered niche, but within this little-known cuisine are product categories that are extremely mainstream. Take samosas, cutlets or even Biryani. Biryani by itself is today a ₹2,500 crore business across organized players, according to a FICCI-PwC report[27]. It's the most ordered item on Swiggy. But

27 FICCI-PWC Report, 'The changing landscape of the retail food service industry', December 2018, http://ficci.in/spdocument/23056/foodzania-release2018.pdf.

that didn't mean that I wanted to disconnect home dining experiences from the home delivery experience entirely. So, I also added our labour-intensive delicacies (think Nalli Nihari, Mutton Khichda, raan), to be pre-ordered by the kilo with a day's notice, to the menu.

Another feature of the home dining experience I wanted to incorporate was the Bohra thaal, which I transformed into a delivery-friendly meal box. Our thaal-inspired box contained one savoury item (appetizer or kharaas), one main course (the jaman—we did Biryani) and, of course, the dessert (meethas). We had an extra spot in the four-compartment tray container, so we added a Kokam Aloo Salad, one of the many accompaniments that you find on a Bohra thaal. To add an experiential twist to it, a note with careful instructions on how one is expected to eat from a thaal, was also included.

I christened this extravagant meal for one, priced at ₹300, Thaal-in-a-Box, and envisioned gamifying the ordering process, allowing diners to customize their kharaas, jaman and meethas selections and home delivering them[28]!

---

28 My vision of the gamified thaal-in-a-box (TIAB) received tremendous validation over a period of time for its innovation in an otherwise bland food delivery space. One great example was when in 2019, UberEats flew me down to their APAC summit in Hong Kong to make a presentation on how I was making regional food mainstream via TIAB. The talk was translated into four languages.

By the second half of 2015, the many opportunities I pursued with Mom in the form of catering small events, food pop-ups at restaurants and delivery, made it evident to me that scaling operations with Mom at the helm was not feasible. For one, it was taking a toll on her physically. Mom is a quiet person, never one to shy away from hard work. When I started conversations with her about setting up a kitchen from which we could start food delivery, she was less than enthusiastic but refrained from voicing her concerns. Finally, when the Pune music fest came around, she had a chat with me about wanting to spend time focusing on home dining experiences and the home in general. In trying to help Mom rediscover her passions, I had taken away the freedom and flexibility she had earned for herself after a lifetime of looking after her family round the clock. She reminded me on several occasions that she was more than happy to train new cooks to help out, but she didn't want to be THE person in charge of the food that left the delivery kitchen every day.

After the Pune debacle, I had it in my head that in order to cook good Bohra food, I needed a good Bohra chef. If Mom wasn't going to be able to take centre stage in my delivery business, I needed someone who understood the nuances of Bohra cooking. In my hunt for the right partner, I asked Dad to speak to any and all the Bohra families he knew who might have a budding chef in their midst. I called family members I hadn't been in touch with for years to check if anyone had developed a vocational talent for cooking Bohra food.

We started the new year of 2016 by introducing operational efficiencies to Mom's cooking. Standardizing Mom's recipes has been one of the greatest challenges of my food delivery business. Finding a well-located, functional kitchen space had seemed like the more difficult task but it paled in comparison to this! Mom had developed her style of cooking using andaaz—estimation—honed over decades of trial and error. But while her intuition guided her, it didn't help in the training of the two young boys who were hired as cooks for TBK's first-ever delivery kitchen. Add to that, Mom can be a very impatient person in the kitchen. I suspect, like most chefs, she does things with a flare that can be hard to replicate. And the new cooks had a lot of questions and took time to keep up with her.

Despite that, Mom somehow managed to not only write down her recipes but also communicate them to the team. To ensure that food from our delivery kitchen tasted of the flavours of home, the masalas used to prepare everything on our menu were still being prepared by her.

Even as this was underway, I had begun the hunt for my cloud kitchen. I had misgivings about licences, rent, pesky landlords without the requisite paperwork, etc., but surprisingly, our first kitchen came easily to us. We found a two hundred square feet space in Worli's BDD chawl; the kitchen was meant to service the area within a five-kilometre radius of Worli for on-demand delivery, and areas beyond that for pre-order items. The kitchen came fitted out with a second-hand domestic fridge, two chulhas and cooking utensils of several different sizes.

From someone who had never set foot in the kitchen while growing up, I was now in charge of preparing an inventory of all things our kitchen would need before we started operations.

Naturally, the first few weeks of operations delivered a series of blows to my confidence. Managing high temperatures in a commercial kitchen was a technical challenge that I was completely unprepared for. The exhaust fan we'd installed wasn't doing the job and those first few weeks were unbearably hot. One of the cooks found an ingenious solution to the problem by taking our standing fan and turning it towards the entryway to direct the hot air away from the kitchen.

We bought a second-hand laptop to manage accounts, inventory and our point of sales (POS) system. Water supply was a recurring problem and water rationed for cooking and cleaning had to be constantly monitored. Another massive expense for the kitchen was the purchase of chairs for the kitchen staff and (occasionally) me. Yes, chairs are pricey. Our internet connection—the backbone of an online food delivery business—wasn't provided by MTNL or Hathway, but by the local cable guy whose reputation was sketchy at best. Our business would come to a screeching halt at least three or four times a week.

If micromanaging the inner workings of my delivery kitchen wasn't task enough, the feedback we were getting for our food was abysmal. The quality wasn't consistent, and the reviews were destroying a year's worth of ten-on-ten ratings that TBK had received for our home dining experiences.

One of the worst reviews came from a customer who had ordered food from us shortly after coming home for lunch. They had rated the food one on five in a Zomato review and expressed their heartfelt disappointment. After reading it, I had the first of many meltdowns; a close friend had to come over and help calm me down.

The two kitchen cooks that I had placed my faith in hadn't a clue about how to fix the problem. They had no idea where they were going wrong! Mom would intervene at these points and monitor the kitchen remotely by speaking to the cooks every day and having them home to go through recipes in person. But for some reason that did little to influence the quality of food leaving the delivery kitchen.

To give you an example of the kind of blunders we made, there was this one time that my brother Mubbasir's father-in-law had pre-ordered a couple of raans from us. Ideally, Mom should have prepared the raan herself to ensure that it was of the highest quality and taste, but I wanted to transition the responsibility to the Worli kitchen team to enable us to cater to higher volumes of such orders.

I may have jumped the gun here. The raan that I confidently sent to uncle was so bad, it was inedible. Over a very polite phone call, he informed me (with the best intentions) that the food wasn't up to the mark and it was far from what guests would expect from a brand like ours.

Another order I recall messing up quite badly was for a lady who wanted to surprise her mother with Bohra food on her birthday. It was a pre-order; my delivery boy landed up at her house a day early, and her mother answered the door. The confused delivery boy called me and handed the phone over to the customer's mother, who was even more perplexed. Amidst this commotion, I realized what we had done. The food went to waste and the surprise was ruined.

My memory is studded with so many such incidents— some grave, some laughable—that occurred in the first few months after we started our delivery service. Over time, I realized that these missteps were hurting the TBK brand, and that my family's reputation was at stake.

On advice from Dad, I decided to simplify production at the Worli kitchen by outsourcing our Biryani to a well-established Bohra caterer. I figured it would let me focus on reviving the brand and food ratings, which in turn would keep the demand for our food up. After a few meetings with the caterer, we reached an arrangement. The caterer's Biryani was getting phenomenal reviews—I now looked forward to making my daily feedback calls every evening!

As the cooks were finally able to focus on the production of pre-order items like raan, khichda and nihari, I had to put some serious thought into creating fantastic packaging and branding for these high-ticket items.

For me, the raan was the hero of the TBK delivery menu. And the takeaway packaging had to represent the cult status that it had acquired in the media and amongst home dining guests. The Legendary Raan in Red Masala was the equivalent of a really good bottle of wine. It was slow-cooked, and the masala was Mom's patent masala mix. A lot of time and effort went into preparing it, and I spent the same on my search for the perfect box for it.

I needed a box that was ten inches in length, thirteen inches in breadth and three inches in height. All that seemed to fit the product description was a cake box. None of the vendors we visited had a ready solution.

That's when it came back to me. Back in my Google days, I had floated a bumper sticker e-commerce venture called Stick It and Go. (What can I say? I'm a restless guy!) I had faced a similar conundrum then—I couldn't find decent packaging to ship the delicate sheets of bumper stickers, so I found a vendor who customized sleek cardboard envelopes for me. There was a minimum order size and additional expenses to create the mould for my very specific box design, but it was well worth it because it didn't take my costs up and storage was simple.

Not so lucky this time around. The minimum order size was five thousand boxes. We were doing about ten raans per week at this point. My kitchen was two hundred square feet small. I couldn't fathom how I would store so many boxes in my tiny kitchen or sell enough raans to use up the customized boxes.

I realized my best bet was to find a temporary ready solution that might take the cost of the raan up, but (hopefully) spark the same thrill as opening the packaging of an iPhone. Dad, who is king of plastics on Sarang Street in Crawford Market, introduced me to a wholesaler who traded in Tupperware-quality boxes. I paid ₹70 to package an item that retailed at ₹1,600. Considering our margins for delivery were wafer-thin, most people in F&B will call me stupid for doing this. I bypassed that line of thinking by referencing some of the most prominent brands that saw value in aligning their product packaging with their brand message. Think of a Fossil watch, nestled in a square tin case with a quirky design that doubles up as a keepsake box.

In short, I was more than happy to justify the obsession that I had with ensuring that our raan was delivered in style. If a guy working at Google with no F&B background whatsoever could venture into selling samosas, my packaging could well mimic what worked for Apple and Fossil. I was thinking outside the box quite literally and I could tell from the customer feedback I got on the raan that the entire experience of being able to order the delicacy, having it delivered in beautiful packaging and consuming it with family or friends, was making an impression.

My days of focusing on packaging came to an end soon enough. Challenges around outsourcing production began cropping up. Consistency wasn't a problem here, which was great. But wastage had increased. Anticipating inventory was proving to be tricky. If we ordered less Biryani, we would have to turn down orders; if we ordered too much, we'd simply have to dispose the Biryani. The cost of the Biryani, coupled with the fee to transport it to our Worli kitchen, was quite high and negotiations around the pricing and supply chain broke down within two months of our partnership.

To be honest, I wasn't fired up at all about pursuing or mending this relationship. I knew that the Biryani we should've been delivering—and would eventually be delivering—had to be produced in our own kitchen.

Soon after, I started the hunt for a head chef who would put their own stamp on the TBK delivery menu and our other signature items. I went through three different chefs over the next few months and singled out the one who could grasp Mom's recipes and was satisfied with the pay that I could afford at the time.

I had found an ustad fit for the job—and not a moment too soon.

While I was trying to sort out the operational challenges staring me in the face, I spent a lot of time during this period apologizing to my customers. I began calling each of them and asking for feedback. First, they would be pleasantly surprised that it's the owner of TBK[29]. They would usually congratulate me on my success and tell me how they had heard about the brand. Then, if required, I

---

29 If there's one thing that's never changed about TBK since the very beginning, it's that people always think we're a much larger business and that I am a lot richer than what is actually the case. In fact, somewhere on the internet, there's a video floating around that talks about my apparent million-dollar net worth. Unfortunately for Zahabia and me, that's not true. Unless this book becomes a bestseller!

would apologize for our goof-up and, if necessary, offer them a complete refund on their order.

I recall putting up a Facebook post apologizing to customers for our terrible performance in one particular week. I was pleasantly surprised by the positive messages I received from our followers. Everyone said one thing—keep at it and please don't give up!

MORE THAN FAILURE BE AFRAID OF NOT TRYING YOUR BEST.

FAIL FAST, AND AS MANY TIMES AS YOU CAN. IT'S A GOOD THING. STRUGGLE FORCES YOU TO THINK ON YOUR FEET AND THAT'S WHY NO ONE HAS MORE POTENTIAL THAN A FAILED ENTREPRENEUR.

8

The Highs Are High, the Lows Are Low

By December 2016, I was broke.

A month earlier, I had been notified by my chartered accountant (CA) that I had outstanding value added tax (VAT) dues that were about to wipe out my entire personal savings account.

I left the meeting in a state of shock. I had spent almost all of 2016 struggling to standardize my food and find a chef, and my accounting responsibilities had taken a backseat. If only I could approach the tax department with that defence.

'Officer, I have been very busy trying to find a chef, customize packaging and standardize our Biryani. Can we please defer our VAT payment to next year once I've had more time to focus on accounting and finance?'

Since that wasn't a real possibility, I shared my situation with a few friends and family members, hoping to get advice or find a possible loophole to defer this liability altogether.

Everyone I spoke to tried to make me feel better about it; privately, though, I'm certain they were wondering how I had neglected such a crucial business compliance. That's the thing about a start-up—you can get so caught up in the day-to-day, that it is actually possible to miss something as obvious as a VAT payment.

I had no choice but to clear my dues and was left to ponder over how I had gone from earning a respectable six-figure salary to not having a stable income and, now, no savings either.

When I quit Google in 2015, I was earning a sizeable annual income with the added bonus of sweat equity in the company. My earnings were mostly savings because I wasn't the kind of person who spent too much on myself. I had a roof over my head—thanks to my parents—and my lifestyle could be termed simple by the standards of most urban twenty-somethings.

This substantial nest egg had enabled me to quit my job and pursue entrepreneurship. I hadn't given myself a salary for over a year because I could afford to live off my savings. With my savings nearly gone, I would have to depend solely on the profits of my still-small enterprise to support myself. It just didn't seem possible.

I truly was ready to call it quits this time. Nothing gives you more perspective than having no money in your bank account.

'Munaf, what's wrong?'

A few days after my visit to the CA's office, my parents found me sitting on my bed crying uncontrollably. They tried their best to console me, even though they hadn't the slightest clue what had triggered this. Neither did I. This was the first time in my life that I had experienced what I termed 'crying fits'. It felt like there was a volcano inside of me all along, on the brink of eruption, and it had finally been set off. I was caught unawares. A few slow, deep breaths allowed me to regain my composure. I was dehydrated and had a splitting headache, and I realized that my parents were terribly shaken. A few hours later, though, it was almost as if nothing at all had happened and I felt like myself again. I brushed it off as one of the many occupational hazards of entrepreneurship and reassured myself and my parents that this was a one-off incident. 'It won't happen again,' I told them.

When I quit my role as senior account strategist to become CEO of TBK, I was well aware of what I was leaving behind and what I was getting into. I knew what I needed from the business, but I didn't know that the business would need something from me too and it wouldn't be just hard work, a salary cut and sleepless nights. I would barter the big gains I made in business with small pieces of my mental well-being which, unchecked over time, would leave me feeling empty on the inside.

The 'crying fits' persisted even after that first episode in 2016. Two years later, I sought therapy and was informed that what I was experiencing ran a lot deeper than just crying fits. It was a physical response to stress, more akin to panic or an anxiety attack than an emotional response alone.

If I thought success was the antidote to feelings of anxiety around the future, I couldn't be further from the truth. In the years ahead, my professional wins and milestones left me feeling worse. How did that work?! Every time something good happened, something big that acknowledged and recognized my effort and business acumen, I grew even more dependent on that feedback to validate myself—not just professionally, but also personally. My business became my identity and I channelled everything that happened with TBK—good or bad, right or wrong—into my own sense of self-worth. Had I caught this early on and talked to someone about it, things might have been different. I knew I was stressed and anxious, but I chalked that up to yet another personal failure instead of seeing it for what it was, a condition that could be easily treated by a professional.

I had friends who were entrepreneurs—my own father was a shining example of a successful self-made businessman himself—but I didn't see anyone else going through what I was. After my third crying fit, I thought to myself, *everyone goes through this, but they handle it better. You need to do the same or TBK is finished!* Now, my stress was stressing me out.

If this wasn't mentally draining enough, there were notable physical symptoms too. I was diagnosed with dermatographic urticaria, a skin disorder with no clear cause (except stress). My body doubled up as a writing board and I itched all over my hands and face when I got too hot. The only solution I found to it was to stress less and pop antihistamines daily to manage the symptoms. I also developed digestion issues—recurring stomach aches and acidity as well as chronic neck pain and headaches. If I was even the least bit vain, I would've given up entrepreneurship entirely. I now sport what is called the salt-and-pepper look (polite speak for premature greying). Lucky for me, my wife digs it!

My experience with stress, anxiety and panic attacks is the story of so many other young founders and seasoned entrepreneurs. The reason why we don't talk about it, write about it, or share it with our family, stakeholders, friends and the world at large is because perception is everything in entrepreneurship. Your business is only as strong as you are. And if you betray any sign of weakness, you may as well shut shop. That's what we're all told in myriad different ways and it's what we inadvertently end up telling each other.

But I am choosing to abandon that narrative for once and say that I wish I had put my mental health above the needs of the business. Yes, I was answerable—both to the investors I've talked about in the chapters ahead, and my employees—but I wish I had found a way to communicate this to them effectively and sought their help in navigating these difficult waters.

By the time the pandemic came around, in 2020, I was seeing a therapist, meditating and exercising regularly. I braced for the impact of this new global development; I thought it would feel like my world was coming to an end. Surprisingly, it didn't.

Being more candid about how I feel and engaging with a mental health professional has perhaps brought about this imperceptible change in how I'm coping with things. It could also be the global pandemic that has brought fresh perspective and a new attitude towards adversity. Maybe it's the fact that I got married earlier this year to the love of my life and I have certainty and stability in the form of a relationship. Or who knows, it could be that the big breakdown is still on the horizon, but I feel alright because I have all the tools that I need to deal with it.

But I'm getting ahead of myself. That day in 2016, I sat on my bed shaking from head to toe, completely overcome by a feeling of helplessness. I wanted to shut TBK down.

Then, something amazing happened.

'Hello, Munaf Kapadia? I'm calling from *Forbes India*.'

I had made the 2017 *Forbes India* 30 under 30 list.

I was stunned and, frankly, a bit annoyed.

I had applied for the list on a pure whim. I had seen the call for entries on my Facebook page. Perusing the online form, I felt like I met the criteria somewhat and decided to apply without thinking too much about it. The process was quick and painless; I didn't expect to be shortlisted.

Just when I was ready to move past this chapter in my life, I found myself stuck. So much so that instead of having any sort of normal reaction—such as gratitude or joy—I responded by asking the caller, 'Why?'

I explained that I was on the verge of shutting the business down. We were not turning huge profits nor was the company's valuation high enough to afford me any kind of recognition. In fact, I had even asked the friend who had joined me to help with operations and finances to exit TBK. Did it make sense for *Forbes India* to still give me the recognition? The response from the other end was something I hold on to even today. The criteria behind shortlisting awardees wasn't only on net worth, but *perceived* worth. They were acknowledging me for the social impact I had made. Their goal was to pick people on the verge of disruption. It didn't matter whether you failed or succeeded, but it did matter that you tried. The call ended with that.

In a way, this win served to validate two years of hard work, grit and incessant relationship building. I thought to myself, *I can't shut TBK down before I appear on the cover of Forbes India. That would be really embarrassing.*

To save me from disgrace, I decided to push myself to keep going for another couple of months.

9

When Ranveer Brar
Compared TBK to a Bicycle

I was on the cover of *Forbes India*!
Of course, I shared that highly coveted spot with Swiggy
co-founders Rahul Jaimini and Nandan Reddy, fashion
designer Masaba Gupta, actor Tahir Raj Bhasin and rower
and Olympic athlete Dattu Bhokanal.

Prior to the photoshoot with photographer Joshua
Navalkar and creative director Anjan Das, I exchanged
a flurry of messages with the designated fashion stylist. I
sent her photos of my entire wardrobe (which isn't saying
much because I am the poster boy for minimalism). On
her advice, I carried practically everything I owned to the
Forbes India office on the day of the shoot. Fortunately, I
had recently bought something formal for my brother's
wedding and it proved to be cover-worthy.

I appeared calm and stoic, but on the inside, I was
wrestling with my anxiety and excitement. I had never

been profiled for a business magazine, nor had I been photographed professionally.

Even though the *Forbes India* team had indicated that my photo had made it to the cover, I waited till it hit the stands for confirmation. It seemed too good to be true, so I kept this news from my family and close friends. I had only informed my immediate circle that I had made it to the Under 30 list.

From the time I learnt about it to the official release date of the list, I worked hard to turn TBK's operations around. I aggressively pushed sales so that we could squeeze a reasonable margin every month just to keep the business afloat.

The day the list was published—2 February 2017— passed in a flash. Dad bought about thirty copies to gift his business associates, our neighbours and family members. My WhatsApp and email were inundated with messages from former co-workers at Google, school friends and home dining guests who had become close acquaintances. It felt like my birthday, but better. I had earned this, and I savoured every second of that day and those that followed.

The pressure of matching up to my newly acquired fame kicked in soon enough. Putting aside my fear and feelings of disillusionment, I felt an urgency to do something big that proved to the world all over again why I was worthy of being put on the cover of *Forbes India*. I had built a powerful brand and succeeded in building the foundation of a delivery business. But I had yet to make substantial commercial gains through TBK.

February 2017: Made the cover of Forbes India. *It felt like my birthday, but better (Photo courtesy* Forbes India).

I could take you through the profit-and-loss sheet of a delivery-only kitchen but instead, I'll run you through the market's expectation of what it takes to run a sustainable food delivery business.

You need to scale-up.

There are two ways to do this—either you operate multiple brands from one single kitchen and set up outlets in relevant catchment areas or you operate a single brand out of a very small kitchen and flood the city with outlets. To succeed at the latter, you need to saturate the market. When you do this, the margins—and therefore, profits—are wafer-thin as it is less revenue per square foot.

The need to monetize my brand—create a store footprint that matched my brand footprint in order to build a sustainable business—was a recurring theme in my conversations with Chef Ranveer Brar.

Ranveer is a recurring character in TBK's story. He was, in fact, the very first celebrity guest at our TBK Home Dining Experience and, till date, Mom's favourite celebrity to work with. His easy charm and genuinely warm personality have made me look forward to conversations and collaborations with him.

Our very first interaction with Ranveer took place in December 2014, when his team reached out to cast TBK on his Living Foodz show titled *The Great Indian Rasoi*. The show covered stories of culture and cuisine across the country, predominantly featuring regional cooking. We had caught his attention within two months of running TBK from Colaba. My parents and I were ecstatic. For Mom, it was the ultimate validation of her cooking. She spent a huge part of her TV time following cookery shows of all kinds, from Tarla Dalal to *MasterChef Australia*. (It wasn't just all saas-bahu shows for her, like I often exaggerate.) Her familiarity with all the celebrity chefs on Indian television made navigating such opportunities so much easier. I could barely tell carrots apart from my toes and I wouldn't recognize a celebrity chef if he showed up outside my house and introduced himself to me! It helped that Mom was able to fully appreciate the visibility we would get out of coverage by someone as well known and well-loved as Ranveer. The fact that Mom is a natural on camera is just another huge plus. All that aside, like every aspiring chef, she was thrilled that the cooking shows she was hooked to watching on television would now feature her!

On the day scheduled for the shoot, Ranveer and his team showed up at home with camera crew, producers and spot boys in tow. It was the first time we were being filmed for television. (This was even before our much-famed BBC shoot in 2015.) We were still very new to the process. As part of the feature, we had to put together a proper sit-down Bohra thaal dinner to give viewers a strong visual of the Bohra thaal dining concept. My parents cajoled a few of our Bohra neighbours and some of their Bohra friends to play actors and extras for the shoot. We even convinced the 'cast' to put on our traditional Bohra attire—saved for visits to the mosque—to apprise audiences of what the average Bohra was expected to dress like. Our community is small and not as widely known as some of the other Islamic offshoots, so we felt it was our responsibility to correctly and proudly depict the Bohra sensibility, customs and heritage.

We had a fantastic experience working with Ranveer on this project. He showed a keen interest in TBK, our food, future plans and Mom's cooking techniques. For someone like me, with no background or connections in the food industry, Ranveer's kind encouragement was motivation to keep TBK's weekend operations going in the early days. I made it a point to share TBK's milestones with him from time to time and would even bump into him at industry events where he would always take time out to catch up with me.

In early 2017, Ranveer launched a vegetarian gourmet restaurant in Kamala Mills, Mumbai. I received an invite for a pre-launch menu tasting at the restaurant.

Despite being immensely busy, being the ever-gracious host that he is, Ranveer committed time to chat with me. I used the opportunity to update him as quickly as possible on what we were up to at TBK.

When I finally took a moment to catch my breath, Ranveer gave me a reassuring look and said, 'Munaf, The Bohri Kitchen is like a bicycle. Your PR and marketing pedal is spinning out of control, while your operations and production pedal is stuck. The business will never move ahead unless both pedals are at pace with one another.'

I was already aware of this. But the analogy he used definitely stuck. I had created a huge demand for Bohra food through TBK. Bohra cuisine was a category that didn't exist independently outside Bohra functions and weddings for the public to access before TBK took off. But I had only two ways of catering to people—one, through home dining on the weekends and, two, through the delivery kitchen in Worli that primarily serviced South Mumbai.

I had invented a great brand and I had also managed to capture the attention of my target audience. The core issue with most businesses that are struggling to grow is usually one or the other. Either you have a brilliant product or service and don't find the right customers/clients because of ineffective marketing and visibility or, as in my case, I had a crystal-clear vision of brand positioning and a steady demand but no solid plan on how to fulfil that demand in the market.

For some time after the conversation, I pondered over whether opening more delivery outlets was the right way to grow TBK. There were other possible avenues that were yet to be explored. For instance, was there a way to scale the TBK Home Dining Experience by creating TBK chapters across the city or even country? Was there a serious opportunity cost to not opening a restaurant for a highly experiential concept like ours? Was there potential for a national chain or QSRs?

The only thing holding me back from exploring all these opportunities was sheer confusion. I knew I had to scale-up but what was the right fit for the brand?

To better understand that, I spent the first few months of 2017 working hard on our operational and production inefficiencies and paid heed to what we were getting right.

I hate to admit it, but my involvement in the operations of my business till the end of 2016 had been minimal. I had brought a partner on board to help set up the delivery kitchen in Worli to take care of production, operations and logistics while I focused on what I did best—marketing, sales and branding. That partnership broke down almost completely in the last months of 2016. I had to reclaim complete charge of production and operations which meant visiting the kitchen every single day, something I hadn't done since I first set it up. Not to mention, the embarrassment of being on the cover of *Forbes India* as CEO and founder of a business that was on the brink of closure kept me motivated to turn things around.

There wasn't enough space in the delivery kitchen for me to sit and work. Every day, after briefing the kitchen staff before we started on lunch deliveries, I would perch on a narrow staircase that led up to the first-floor kitchen, open my laptop and make my calls. At that hour, I could hear the TV blaring or the loud chatter of residents in the tenements below. There were a small posse of chickens that belonged to one of our neighbours that would boldly flap around the area below.

There were days when I found this work exhilarating; on some days, I couldn't help but think that only a year ago, I was seated at a plush office in front of a laptop managing the advertising accounts of the top financial institutions in the country. Now, I was counting chickens.

This line of thought began to wane after the *Forbes India* cover. I now had a thorough understanding of what went on in our delivery kitchen, what we were getting right, where there was scope for improvement and the potential for profit, production and expansion.

In April 2017, I began thinking about raising investment for TBK. Up until this point, I had been using my savings to fund the business. The small-scale delivery operations we were running out of Worli was profitable but being a cloud or delivery-only kitchen, it didn't generate the kind of revenue that the business needed to seed another ten outlets across the city. If we were unable to scale to at least ten outlets, then the kind of outreach the brand had managed to establish would be completely wasted.

I've elaborated on the process of fundraising in the chapters to come, but what I did start doing simultaneously (while speaking to my investment banker friends and founders of other food start-ups) is figure out how I wanted to build out my operations if I were to open ten to fifteen outlets across Mumbai. So far, TBK had succeeded on the back of its small scale and nicheness. We started with home dining experiences and then a small delivery kitchen, and that was all we did for a period of three years from inception. We had slowly and cautiously also ventured into catering. But at the back of my mind, I knew that my decision to quit Google was based on a broader vision for both home dining experiences and TBK. Since plans for TDT had to be shelved, I needed TBK delivery to grow beyond its South Mumbai radius and reach all the people in the city who had heard about us.

Having that conversation with Ranveer was a turning point for me because it pushed me to rethink my approach to keeping up with the demand my PR tactics were creating. I had to scale. I also had to do it through delivery since that was the business model I had chosen to focus on outside of our home dining experiences.

When I quit Google, I knew I'd be letting go of great growth prospects, a lot of perks and enviable pay, but I also left with the conviction that I would make it up to myself by creating a legacy to leave behind.

I'm determined to make my mark.

FALL IN LOVE
WITH YOUR
BUSINESS IDEA
BUT GET MARRIED
TO THE IDEA OF
ENTREPRENEURSHIP.

COMMIT TO THE MINDSET
BUT DON'T BE STUCK
ON THE IDEA THAT YOU
STARTED OUT WITH.

10

Goddess of TBK Meets the Stars

Early in 2015, reporters always asked me, 'What is your vision for The Bohri Kitchen?'

My MBA brain was tempted to say, 'Open a restaurant someday!' or 'Get more Bohra families to pursue home dining!'

Instead, I responded with, 'I want Shah Rukh Khan to come home, my family and I are big fans.' Did I really want SRK to come home? Of course! But I intuitively felt that our Bollywood dreams would be more interesting to read about than my 'business plan' for TBK.

But how does one get Bollywood to your doorstep or how do you get to theirs?

TBK's first encounter with Bollywood happened in March 2017, a month after I made the *Forbes India* cover. Coincidentally, the same gentleman who gave Shah Rukh Khan his Bollywood breakout performance gave us ours. It started with a conversation with my friend's mother, who asked me to 'expect a call from Adi'.

The name didn't ring any bells, but I said, 'Sure, I'll speak to him.' Later that day, I did get a call from a man who identified himself as Adi and asked if we would do the catering for his wife's birthday. At this time, we hadn't started doing the thaal experience (what we have now dubbed the 'Travelling Thaal') in the form of private caterings or even thought about it seriously. I promptly said no, but I reiterated that we would be happy to host him, his wife and their guests at my home in Colaba.

Later that evening, my friend's mother called me again and was surprised to hear that I had turned down an opportunity to cater for THE Aditya Chopra and Rani Mukerji.

I was stunned. I had no idea that Aditya Chopra went by Adi. I rang him back, still unsure whether we could cater a thaal dining experience in someone else's home, let alone a high-profile client. But then again, if we had to push ourselves to do it, it may as well have been for Aditya Chopra. Adi and I spoke briefly about TBK, raan and samosas when, quite unexpectedly, he asked me to drop by his place so that we could meet in person to finalize the menu and I could recce the venue[30].

Till then, I had never seen the inside of a Bollywood celebrity's home and all it had taken was a ten-minute phone conversation to make it happen for the first time!

---

30 Which was to satisfy myself that the thaal would fit through his front door.

If this wasn't exciting enough, I decided to take Zahabia—who I was dating at the time—to Adi's house since we had plans to meet that evening. It was early days in our relationship (Zahabia and me, not Adi!) and I was wary of cancelling on her. I didn't bother informing Zahabia that we were going to Aditya Chopra's house, knowing fully well that she would think she wasn't dressed for it. She'd either refuse to come in or insist on going home and changing first. I simply told her that I had to drop by a client's house for a quick meeting. It was only after we were sitting inside the Chopras' living room, and Adi and Rani joined us, that Zahabia realized whose house it was.

Over the course of that meeting, while Zahabia sat there tongue-tied, all my preconceived notions about the film industry and the high-handed attitude and tantrums of its members diminished considerably. I wanted to go back home with stories of extravagance, flamboyance and high drama, but it turned out to be a routine client-vendor meeting with perhaps the most down-to-earth people I have had the pleasure of doing business with. I quickly took Adi, and later Rani, through the menu and did a look-see of the space that they would be using to host their guests. Barring a small debate on whether guests should be made to eat directly from the thaal or given individual plates, the meeting wrapped up in record time.

The catering for Rani's birthday went off without a hitch. I had decided that Mom would lead production for the event, even though at this point we had a full-fledged kitchen team that could handle it. I was a bundle of nerves the night before, but my ever-cool mother talked me down in a way that only she could, stating with some authority that our celebrity guests were no different from the ones we hosted every weekend in our home. And our weekend events were a solid ten on ten.

With that we went on to successfully cater our first proper Travelling Thaal experience to celebrate Rani Mukerji's birthday. To ensure that the dining experience came as close to what we did at home, we served two thaals—one vegetarian, the other non-vegetarian. Guests served themselves from the thaal, but used individual plates.

One of my favourite memories from that meal was how it started out with everyone making fun of the vegetarians who had their own separate thaal. Yet, by the end of the meal, all the non-vegetarians were gorging on the vegetarian food as well! Another wonderful outcome of this association was becoming acquainted with Aditya Chopra's mother, Pam aunty. Till date, she remains a big fan of our smoked samosas and continues to evangelize TBK in the sincerest way possible. God bless aunty!

Catering Adi's party confirmed two things—(a) TBK's thaal experience retained customer satisfaction, food quality and the experiential aspects of home dining even outside our home and (b) it elevated our home dining experiences from a niche, rustic concept to a glamorous, highbrow affair.

After I uploaded a photo of Mom and Rani from the night of the dinner, I received a call from a journalist asking for details of the event. They wanted to know everything, from the guest list to the menu and any gossip that I would be willing to share. I was tempted to talk about the family members and friends who had shown up, the inside jokes and meal preferences or even the warm conversations between Mom and Rani. I knew it was all PR gold. But this was not how I wanted to build the TBK brand, at the expense of my clients' private lives. TBK will grow and become famous not at the cost of our customers, but because of our customers.

I called Adi and asked him what I should do. He said, quite sweetly, 'Munaf, if it helps your business, please go ahead and share details of the menu but leave everything else to the readers' imagination.' The PR we generated was phenomenal! The engagement on social media surpassed anything we had received before.

In short, the Aditya Chopra magic that catapulted Shah Rukh to fame did the same for us too.

A short while later, filmmaker Rahul Rawail, whose son worked with Adi, made a catering enquiry with us and we did a Travelling Thaal for him as well. He was so pleased with the entire experience, he offered to put in a good word for us within his close circle of family and friends.

As much as I harp on about the value of good branding and being PR-savvy, word of mouth and goodwill has played an immeasurable role in making TBK popular. It's indisputably the best kind of PR there is because it's honest. It also instils the kind of shameless confidence that is required to randomly go up to someone and invite them home for a meal.

One night, when I was out to dinner at a suburban eatery, I spotted Farah Khan with a few friends. I thought to myself, *there's no harm in going up to her and inviting her home for a meal. I'm sure she's been accosted in public for a lot worse.* I walked up to Farah, offered her my business card and informed her that my family and I were BIG fans! She was kind enough not to swat me away for interrupting her during a meal. After that night, I pushed the incident to the back of my mind. Farah, however, did not forget.

She contacted me a few months later and asked when she could come home for the TBK Home Dining Experience. We set a date, and I immediately called Mom to make sure that she was available for a closed dinner. With Bollywood films being my family's biggest weakness after food, my parents were overjoyed to host her.

We planned a feast, putting together a 'Best of TBK' menu featuring our raan, khichda, Dum Biryani, Smoked Mutton Kheema Samosas, Russian Cutlets and hand-churned ice cream.

The TBK company line is that we treat all our guests like movie stars or, at least, that's how my parents do things. Ironically, TBK is also the place where movie stars are made to feel completely relaxed and—might I add—normal, thanks to how easy going and completely unassuming my parents are. It takes them exactly ten minutes to forget who their guests are (no matter how famous) and start being their usual selves.

The evening that Farah and her party came over was a dream. This was the very first time a Bollywood celebrity had set foot in our house. Our kitchen had never seen this grand a variety of food being prepared, all on the same day either. If the first few moments of ushering everyone in, and greeting our guests, was a tad bit awkward, it was soon forgotten. The rest of the evening went by like it was a dinner with old friends. The battle of wits that ensued between Dad and Farah is unforgettable—we laugh about it even today. It proved, once and for all, that no one escapes Dad's cutting humour, not even Farah Khan.

Farah has gone down as one of TBK's most cherished guests. Her down-to-earth personality, graciousness and effervescence have made her a friend more than a VIP[31] client of TBK. Six months after she came home, she got in touch to request raan and samosas for her birthday celebration. That week, we had a double whammy because none other than Hrithik Roshan called, asking us to cater his birthday dinner at his home!

Still finding our legs in the catering business, I was unrelenting in ensuring every single event was executed seamlessly. Despite this, so many small things would go wrong. It was the genuine warmth, understanding and appreciation of guests at this time that would help us through it.

---

31 Her contact is saved as (TBK-VIP) Farah Khan; (TBK-Effervescence) would take up too much space.

Farah brought along Ashutosh Gowariker and his wife Sunita, which was an added bonus.

I vividly recall how, on the evening of Farah's birthday, we were badly delayed. I was making the delivery myself because I wanted to make sure the order reached her in perfect condition. I had left home in the nick of time only to find myself stuck in the worst rush hour traffic ever. Realizing that I may very well reach Farah's house after her party was over, I redirected my cab to the nearest train station and hopped on to a crowded Mumbai local with two tapelas in hand, only to reach an hour late.

I was mortified, but Farah didn't lose her cool or even bring up the delay. Instead, she invited me to join the revelry and happily took me around her living room, introducing me to her guests. I pride myself at holding my own and playing it cool around the most famous personalities, but I was totally out of my comfort zone that night. I was visibly star-struck. Karan Johar couldn't have cared less when Farah introduced me to him and Shilpa Shetty[32] made it clear that our food would be highly incompatible with her diet. Abhishek Bachchan probably looked right through me (can't blame him, he's really that tall). But I was absorbing that evening like a sponge. Incidentally, Vishal Dadlani was also present that evening at Farah's house. He had been a judge on the reality TV show *Grilled*[33], which I had participated in (and won! That story's coming up). I had gotten to know him quite well on the show and that night at Farah's house, he was kind enough to engage me in a conversation and save me from having to lurk around with no company.

The experience catering for Hrithik was similar. He gave us access to his staff, kitchen and whatever else we needed to execute the dinner smoothly. We were made to feel like guests! In 2020, we catered his birthday again and went on to do another event for his parents in that year.

---

32 Shilpa was someone we really wanted to invite because Mom worships her because of all the reality shows she judges. Somewhere in this book you will find how the universe finally made the meeting happen!

33 Yes, I was in a food entrepreneur-based reality show on Fox Life called *Grilled*. More details in later chapters.

At the expense of tooting my own horn, my style is a notch above the detached coolness of catering managers who focus on making themselves and their staff as invisible as possible. We're warm and passionate at TBK, and the experience is as much about the people serving as it is about the food. It's one of the advantages of a small business—you get to be involved, get your hands dirty and on occasion, hang out with Hrithik Roshan himself.

We were treated on par with the guests when we catered Hrithik's party at his home.

Of all the celebrity guests that I expected to come home for a meal, I could never have imagined hosting Rishi Kapoor. In September 2017, I had been invited to address students at an engineering college in Chembur. Minutes before I was to get on stage, my phone buzzed, and an unknown number flashed on the screen. I hate skipping calls from unknown numbers since I'm always passing my business cards around and an unanswered call could mean a missed business opportunity. I asked the organizers for a quick second to take the call.

On the other end of the line, a man said, 'Main sir ko phone de raha hoon.'

Then I heard the unmistakable rich baritone that could only belong to Rishi Kapoor. 'Hello, is this Munaf?'

He told me that Rahul Rawail had recommended TBK to him[34] and asked if I could come over for a quick meeting at his residence in Bandra right away. After the talk, I made my way to Mr Kapoor's home. He greeted me warmly at the door and took me to his guest room where his wife Neetu Kapoor joined us. We spoke casually about everything under the sun. Finally, we arrived at the event at hand, the menu, my recommendations, logistics, etc.

The request was not for catering but delivery of our food. Anyhow, I made sure Mom made the food herself and she was more than happy to—Rishi Kapoor being her childhood heart-throb. The food was to be delivered by me to ensure that everything was reheated, plated and served properly by their staff. The delivery was slated for 26 September 2017, a day Mumbai experienced one if its worst rains. I remember the authorities closed the Bandra-Worli Sea Link—it was that bad.

---

34 Word of mouth is a beautiful, slow but sure thing. A good five months after the Rahul Rawail catering, Mr Kapoor called!

I reached the venue a good three hours prior and perched myself on a stool in the kitchen, playing video games on my phone till it was time for service. Rishi uncle waltzed in and offered me a drink, which I politely refused, but we did have an invigorating conversation on the state of F&B in India and the influence of artificial intelligence in our day-to-day lives.

As the guests started to arrive, I busied myself with supervising service. I saw Ranbir approach me as I was carrying a plate of freshly fried samosas and I assumed he was making a beeline for them. Imagine my surprise when he said, 'Hi Munaf! I'm Ranbir, just wanted to say hello and that I've heard a lot about you!' He went on to elaborate how, on his way to the gathering, he was accompanied by a common friend, Anirban Blah, who told him all about TBK and how we came to be.

A few weeks after the event at Rishi uncle's house, the unimaginable happened. The grand success of our catering brought Rishi Kapoor home for our signature TBK experience and he brought along a surprise guest—food critic, columnist and a revered force on the Indian F&B scene, the wonderful Rashmi Uday Singh. It was a surreal moment for all of us in the Kapadia household. My parents were reliving their childhood!

The next day, there was a half-page article in *The Bombay Times* by Rashmi with a photo of Mr Kapoor flanked by my parents, Rashmi and myself. Rashmi then went on to create a Best Bohri Food Category under the Times Food Awards (now Times Food and Nightlife Awards), a testament to just

Mom was thrilled to cook for her childhood heart-throb
Mr Rishi Kapoor.

how well-appreciated our food and home dining experience was. TBK went on to win the award in 2018 and 2019 as well. I found it surreal that we didn't even have a brick-and-mortar outlet, we fed numbers in the early double digits every weekend and yet, we were amongst a list of awardees that each served hundreds of customers, every day.

Our spate of Bollywood dinner guests also included the elusive and uber-talented Sanjay Leela Bhansali. I think calling myself a fan of his won't suffice. I am in awe of his brilliant movies and understated demeanour. Going by Mr Bhansali's cinematic sensibilities, my parents and I expected dinner to be a quiet and serious affair. I would even go so far as to say that my parents were slightly nervous about hosting someone as revered as Mr Bhansali. To our astonishment, he and his family turned out to be a jovial lot! They made themselves extremely comfortable in our home, putting us at complete ease from the get-go.

I was so fascinated by how they let their guard down completely that it made me protective, almost possessive, about the concept of home dining. It wasn't an attempt at recreating a restaurant. It was an entity of its own, a non-judgemental, safe and inviting space that provided a level of intimacy and community that was unmatched in the F&B industry.

We had another rather unexpected celebrity guest interaction at one of our TBK Home Dining Experiences.

It was a regular weekend lunch and we were doing things as per routine when I noticed one unusual guest. A pretty, young woman who was still wearing her sunglasses even after being seated and helping herself to a beverage in our living room. She didn't take them off when the first course was served. She left them on till the very end of the meal.

At some point during the service, Dad took me aside and asked me, quite seriously, 'Isn't the lady in the sunglasses an actor?' Now, Dad isn't exactly a rubbernecker. He loves watching movies, but his memory for the younger lot of actors today is non-existent. Even if he remembers the face, he'd never recognize them by name, let alone ethnicity. Imagine my intrigue when he confidently said, 'She's that half-Bohra actor!'

It made perfect sense that Dad would recognize her, of course. She was half Bohra! It was none other than Aditi Rao Hydari seated in our living room.

Zahabia didn't know, but I had the biggest crush on Aditi. She looked even better in person. I kept my excitement in check, since she was clearly going to great lengths to avoid attracting any attention and I could respect that. When she finally got up to wash her hands, I very discreetly confirmed her identity by asking her upfront. She responded politely and then happily chatted away with Mom in the kitchen.

At times like this, just like everyone else, I'm incredibly tempted to ask for a selfie or a social media mention, but I fight the urge. Instead, I busied myself with wrapping up the lunch that afternoon. Later that evening, after everyone had left and my parents and I had finished our lunch, I received a notification on Instagram that Aditi—with her four million-plus followers—had tagged TBK with a photo of Mom captioned 'Goddess of TBK!'

It's always a sweet experience to have celebrities eat our food but it's even sweeter when that guest happens to be a fellow Cathedralite! Actor, sportsman and writer Rahul Bose has not only ordered food from us in the city but has also found a way to take our legendary raan to the Andamans. The quality checks that we *ran* that raan through would've given Milkha Singh a *run* for his money. I'm guessing Rahul thoroughly enjoyed the raan out in the Andamans because when I invited him to the launch of our very first brick-and-mortar outlet at Flea Bazaar Café (a concept food court), he very graciously attended.

Catering to celebrity clients has taught my team and me a lot about flexibility in customer service. Their requests sometimes tend to be unconventional; if you screw up, you may lose face with them for good, but if you figure out how to deliver on those requests, you gain loyalists for a lifetime. Our celebrity guests have tested our operational limits which has enabled us to serve all our clients better and set higher standards for ourselves. Thanks to Rahul, we are able to produce, pack and process our chutneys, samosas and Biryanis in a way that enables customers to carry them overseas. If we can send raan on a plane, our other items could very well travel first class!

Bollywood wasn't just coming home or asking us to cater, they were also loyal patrons of our delivery business. Every once in a while, I'd get a call from an unknown number and thank my stars that I picked up because it would be Deepika Padukone or Huma Qureshi requesting Biryani or haleem from our kitchen. If the Page 3 mentions on TBK's popularity among the B-town crowd wasn't enough elation, Mom's obvious joy and excitement at having characters from her TV screen land up in her living room made me appreciate the Bollywood connection even more.

It's been a personal high for me to watch Mom receive the kind of acknowledgement she has from people she so admires. In a lot of ways, it's been the highest of highs of the TBK journey, because before we started out with TBK, my family and I barely thanked her for the meals she prepared daily, no matter how extravagant they were. And here we had people she would've only dreamt of interacting with, enjoying her food and giving her phenomenal feedback on her cooking.

When I sit down to take stock of all the publicity that TBK has received in its short lifespan without even being a real restaurant, without having a PR agency on board and without any personal connections to anyone in the film industry or any industry for that matter, I realize what a powerful tool branding can be. And while feeding Bollywood did wonders for our PR, it also pushed us to explore our strengths and closely evaluate the potential for the bigger brand collaborations that we went on to do in the years to come.

One of the few perks (there aren't too many) of being in the F&B space is that you get to meet people from all walks of life. That relationship only gains more depth when you're hosting them for a meal in your home. And that relationship comfortably acquires the steadiness of friendship when an entire family takes time out to give you the best Bohra meal of your life.

11

Thrilled I Won *Grilled*

In August 2017, I got a call from Victor Tango, a production house that was making a reality TV show for Fox Life called *Grilled*.

I'll be very honest. I didn't take that call seriously at all.

I was in the midst of raising my first round of funding for TBK and reality TV wasn't my idea of PR anyway. It was so far out of anything I had imagined for myself or the brand that I hadn't evaluated the opportunity cost of not doing it. More importantly, the initial description about the show sounded like it was a play off between chefs to win prize money to open their own restaurants. I could at best make an omelette.

I jokingly shared this news with a few close friends and was quite surprised that a lot of them encouraged me to do it!

I was told that it would do great things for my credibility and personal brand (in terms of visibility) and that would inspire confidence in potential investors to hedge their bets on TBK. Also, airtime on TV is easily the most expensive kind of marketing, and I would get that for free and be allowed to pitch my business!

I was still quite reluctant, but when I got a follow-up call from the production house asking me to come in for a screen test and meet the crew, I agreed. At the first meeting, I was given a low-down on the concept of the show, expectations from the channel and producers and, most importantly, who the co-contestants and judges would be. When they told me that the show was not just about cooking (like *MasterChef*) but also your entrepreneurial skills in setting up and executing your business plan (like *Shark Tank*), I was able to visualize myself doing it.

When they revealed that Riyaaz Amlani was one of the judges, that sealed the deal!

Founder of Impresario, a ₹350 crore-hospitality chain[35] behind some of the most exciting F&B concepts in India such as SOCIAL and Smoke House Deli, Riyaaz was someone I had always looked up to. After launching TBK, I had grand plans to place our Smoked Mutton Kheema Samosas at SOCIAL outlets across the city.

In April 2016, after a lot of chasing, I had finally managed to track him down.

---

35 'Impresario to raise $50 million to ramp up restaurant business', *The Hindu*, 25 June 2019.

'Hi, is this Riyaaz?' I said, a little surprised that he answered on my first try.

'Yes, how can I help you?' he said.

'This is Munaf Kapadia. I'm the Chief Eating Officer of The Bohri Kitchen. I was wondering if it would interest you to introduce TBK samosas on your menu at SOCIAL?'

We were barely doing ₹30 lakh in annual sales at that time. That's 0.1 per cent of Impresario's numbers.

'Oh nice! I've heard about you! Can you come over to Khar SOCIAL right now?'

I took a train from Churchgate to Khar and ninety minutes later, I had met Riyaaz. He asked me to get back to him with rates for the samosas that ensured SOCIAL maintained their margins.

That night itself I sent him the rates and waited anxiously for a reply that never came. I sent him a couple of WhatsApp messages but never heard back. I convinced myself that I had lost my shot at collaborating with one of the largest F&B tycoons in the country.

Then I did something impulsive.

I called up an acquaintance who worked for him and asked if he had any idea where Riyaaz might be at that very moment. He had heard, on the grapevine, that Riyaaz was at the Todi Mills SOCIAL.

There was no guarantee that Riyaaz would be there and even if he was, there was no reason why he would meet me. Still, I got there in sixty minutes.

I entered the Todi Mills compound gate and saw him standing right there! I told the driver to stop, but he just kept going. God bless the crazy traffic at the gate, it gave me the few minutes I needed to roll down the window, wave frantically at Riyaaz and ask whether he was headed out. He indicated that I should wait for him at SOCIAL.

'Hey, where's Riyaaz sitting?' I asked the manager at the outlet. I parked myself next to his table and after he was done with his pre-planned meetings, he finally sat down beside me.

'So, what's up, Munaf?' he said.

After haggling a bit, we agreed to take the collaboration aka TBK Samosas@SOCIAL ahead.

For the first time in my life, I had to deal with the logistics of dispatching thousands of samosas at a time. I also learnt (the hard way) that damaged goods can eat into your carefully calculated margins and why cold chain logistics are important. On the positive side, the product was a hit![36]

Shooting for *Grilled* was surreal. Being on a TV set day in and day out for two weeks straight, participating in a cooking show when I didn't know how to cook and leaving my delivery business to be managed entirely by a team that

---

36 We added an experiential component to it by placing a flag on each plate which had instructions on how to eat a TBK samosa. You bite off a corner, add some lemon to activate that smoky flavour and apply some coriander chutney for good measure!

was new, was difficult for me. In retrospect, I am glad I did it, because not only did I go on to win the show—and get Riyaaz Amlani on board as an investor—I also gained an incredible amount of publicity for my personal brand, an asset that I had neglected. I later realized what an important role it played when it came to fundraising.

The two weeks felt like eternity. Crashing at fellow contestant and Pack a Pav founder Rohan Mangalorkar's house, gorging on Goila Butter Chicken Rolls for dinner, getting to know the other contestants and their respective food journeys or simply preparing for the next challenge. I would have said it was all fun—except it wasn't. Managing TBK remotely was a nightmare. I remember thinking that the draw of being on a reality TV show to do something good for my business might actually be the reason why it shuts down!

There were many hilarious anecdotes I can recall from the filming of the show, only most of them were deeply embarrassing for me. My saas-bahu moment (the camera zooming in-and-out of my face, complete with sound effects) came when I couldn't spell a-v-o-c-a-d-o or when Riyaaz chose to take my case for not knowing the difference between sparkling and still water. Also, if you do ever find yourself watching *Grilled* on Hotstar, don't miss how incredibly inconsistent my moustache is. It had a life of its own, choosing to be up or down depending on my fortune in that episode.

Me being grilled on *Grilled*.

Since the inception of TBK, we have gone from strength to strength where the brand's PR, outreach and visibility were concerned. I have made the cover of *Forbes India*, featured in *Conde Nast Traveller* and *Entrepreneur* magazines. TBK is a two-time winner of the Times Food Award. Mom has been recognized as the Best Home Chef of the Year (2018) by the Indian Restaurant Congress. We won the Rising Star award at *Mid-Day*'s The Guide Restaurant Awards 2018; Mom was thrilled to receive the award from Shilpa Shetty Kundra, one of her favourite Bollywood actors!

My family and I would like to take all the credit for making the brand what it is today. But the truth is, we've had a lot of support along the way.

Immediately after the first write-up on TBK appeared in the online newsletter Brown Paper Bag, Ranveer Brar featured us on his show. In the following month, Ranveer tweeted about TBK to Chef Sanjeev Kapoor. You can only imagine how that exploded on our social media pages!

Our next break came in July 2015, when we did an interview with RJ Hrishikesh Kannan—Hrishi K—for Radio One Mumbai.

This was a big milestone for me because Radio One is my go-to radio station. I had tried a hundred different ways to reach out to Hrishi K, and all of them were unsuccessful. Then one day, I was in a car and I heard him on the radio encouraging his listeners to tweet to him who their greatest inspiration was and why. This was a competition, and the winner would get tickets to the TEDx Gateway event at the National Centre for the Performing Arts (NCPA).

While I wanted to attend the TEDx talk[37], I was really excited to have this opportunity to connect with Hrishi K and invite him for a meal at my place. I tweeted, 'My mom is my greatest inspiration, for the manner in which she transformed from housewife to mom chef at The Bohri Kitchen.' I won the tickets and got Hrishi K's number. A

---

37 This was the first TEDx event I had ever attended and as I listened to the fantastic stories being told, I dreamt of being on that stage myself. As I write this, I've been fortunate enough to have spoken at four TEDx talks.

few WhatsApp forwards later, my family was invited for an interview at the Radio One studio!

The acknowledgement and praise for what we had created gave me a much-needed confidence boost, and also reassured my parents (to some extent) that I hadn't made the worst decision of my life quitting Google.

When I was three months into working for TBK full-time, I was contacted by BBC News in November 2015. They were creating short feature segments on regional cuisines across Asia and wanted to shoot TBK for their show *Global Pulse*. I couldn't have responded any faster. This was a dream! The very idea that there would be people sitting in a different corner of the world, who had probably never been to India, but would now discover Bohra food and learn about my business and the family behind it. I was overjoyed with this news as were my parents.

The BBC shoot was a revelation in videography and filmmaking. The crew comprised exactly three people— Vlad Jakovlev, Ieva Ludviga and Amit Vachharajani—and they were smart and organized. Initially they intended to only cover a few Bohra food courses made by Mom to create maybe a minute of actual video content.

They couldn't have known TBK is a little bit like a Venus flytrap. Instead of flies, we devour journalists! Just swap the eating of the fly with convincing a reporter to turn a small paragraph into a full-page spread with colour photographs for a weekend edition!

Vlad and Ieva had to change their plans once we convinced them about the full scope of TBK. Eventually, the shoot turned into a two-day roller-coaster ride comprising an actual home dining experience and trailing Dad on his weekly visit to Colaba market. This video, which captured some beautiful moments, was telecast across the world on 15 August a year later. (The crew tried creating a 360-degree shot of the thaal by installing seven GoPro cameras on the fan above it. A creative, but not very successful idea!)

Gradually, Mom and I became proficient at being in front of the camera. The next two years were filled with opportunities that came in the form of interviews, cooking presentations and video bytes on Bohra food that were all recorded for consumption via radio, press, television or even digital.

One way to summarize my approach towards marketing TBK is that I never took the brand too seriously. This allowed me an agility in the collaborations that I did which astounded our fans. At one point in time, I convinced Uber to activate a coupon code called BOHRIFOODCOMA[38]. The goal with our brand positioning was to simply entertain the consumer, whether they have come home to eat or are consuming our content on social media.

---

38 After eating Mom's food, many of our guests pivot from their original plan to go home by train and Uber it instead. We once had a guest who fell asleep on the marble floor in our living room. I literally rolled him out of my house. We call this phenomenon Bohri Food Coma (BFC); it's also my Wi-Fi password.

I would be over-simplifying my PR strategy if I said that all I did was churn out a great menu, write some witty one-liners on social media, send WhatsApp broadcasts intermittently and give a few talks. I had to continue finding ways to keep TBK exciting for myself and for the customer. One such route was on the shoulders of existing brands. This got the ball rolling for collaborations which the press and average Mumbai foodie would find pleasantly surprising.

In July 2016, we collaborated with Woodside Inn to launch the Raan Burger as part of their burger festival. We had learnt a lot from our operations managing the SOCIAL collaboration and this time around we nailed the supply chain, sending frozen marinated raan to their Colaba and Andheri restaurants. Despite being the most expensive burger on the menu, we were the second-highest selling burger in the festival!

One of our most successful collaborations had to be the Iftar meal at Magazine Street Kitchen in June 2017. We went all out with our 'Mother of all Feasts' menu, selling seventy seats at ₹3,500 per head in a matter of a week. The guests were seated on a carpet and served on a traditional Bohra thaal. Another favourite brand tie-up was with BAR BAR, a cool concept restaurant by Romil Ratra, which introduced our Thaal-in-a-Box on their menu. Instead of a plastic container, they served the food in a tiffin box. Again, an amazing experience sending fresh food daily to Kurla.

While it has been Mom's dream that TBK becomes so famous that Shah Rukh Khan lands up at our doorstep, it was my dream that we become so respected that the great Taj Mahal hotel—that almost never hosts pop-ups by external brands—chose to make an exception for TBK.

In the last week of August 2019, we did a week-long Bohra thaal takeover at the prestigious Masala Kraft at The Taj Mahal Palace Hotel, Colaba. With Mom overseeing the food preparation in the kitchens, we had a chance to work with THE best hospitality team in the city. We placed a limited edition TBK menu along with the Masala Kraft menu and even managed to squeeze in a thaal experience for guests who were so inclined.

The amazing thing about dreams is, when they finally come true, you get to replace them with new ones. My sights are now set on hosting a Bohra thaal pop-up in a foreign country. And we're still waiting for SRK to call!

THE SMARTEST WAY TO HELP YOURSELF IS BY ASKING FOR HELP.

AS AN ENTREPRENEUR, YOU'RE ONLY AS LONELY AS YOU WANT TO BE. LOOK AROUND YOU: EVERYONE'S DYING TO BE A PART OF YOUR JOURNEY.

12

Raise Fun, Not Funds

When I first broached the topic of raising funds to expand TBK's business with Dad, his response was, 'What are you giving them in return?'

'Equity,' I said, to which pat came the reply, 'What's the interest rate?'

Jokes aside, equity is the most expensive way to raise capital. While there is no fixed interest rate, there is a fixed long-term interest in your business. In exchange for the cash flow, you are granting your investors a permanent role in your decision-making process.

This wasn't very clear to me in 2017 when I first stepped into the universe of fundraising and private equity to grow TBK's delivery business and launch small experience centres as an extension to our home dining experience (more on that later). I didn't have a background in finance, and I think you may have sensed by now that accounting is my Achilles' heel. I was confident about my ability to pitch to investors but was unsure about what happened if

I was successful at it. I had tried raising funds in 2015 for TDT, but that had been a one-shot effort at raising a small investment that I eventually didn't accept.

With no clear plan or objective, I made two calls.

The first one was to Apoorv Ranjan Sharma, an acquaintance of mine who runs a start-up accelerator called Venture Catalyst. They advise and manage funds for some of the top high-net-worth individuals (HNIs) and family businesses across the country. Apoorv had shown interest in backing TDT, but I didn't go ahead with raising funds at that point in time. I vaguely recalled him telling me that if ever I decided to raise funds for TBK, I should call him. In 2017, I did, and he sounded excited to hear about my plans. We set up a meeting for the following week.

The conversation with Apoorv had me pumped, so I immediately made the second call to Googler-turned-investment banker Mihir Mehta. It's important that you get to know Mihir a little before I tell you about that phone call. We had first met on the Google campus in Hyderabad, and we reconnected once we both quit the company. He was an investment banker at Ashika Capital, and I was eating and selling samosas at TBK. When I rang Mihir, it had been a while since we had last spoken so I was a bit hesitant about asking him for help. Mihir, on the other hand, seemed more than happy to offer advice even when I informed him that he'd be getting paid in Mom's Smoked Tur Dal Samosas.

I'm glad that I met Mihir before I met anyone else, including the folks at Venture Catalyst. A very brief conversation between us quickly revealed that (a) I needed an investment banker and (b) I needed to put myself and the company through a discovery process to arrive at some pretty basic stuff.

Did I want to give equity in my company to investors?

Did I want to raise debt?

Did I have a rough estimate on my valuation?

How much money did I need and what exactly did I need it for?

Did I want to go the VC route when there were other, simpler options like asking close family and friends to invest?

After this point, Mihir basically became my BFF.

At this meeting, not only did he offer to become de facto investment banker, representing TBK and me to investors, but he also showed an interest in investing in the business himself. Considering Mihir is vegetarian, had had one conversation with me on the topic of fundraising and full knowledge of how little I knew about private equity, I'd say that he was either completely foolish or genuinely believed in my brand.

I took Mihir with me for the preliminary meeting with Venture Catalysts or V Cats, as I'll be referring to them from here on. Apoorv expressed great confidence in the brand, story and business plans that I had charted out. We discussed numbers and agreed to meet again when we had something to show them in the form of a pitch.

When Mihir and I put together the valuation of the company, we factored in sales, annual revenue, expenses, unit economics, etc. There was a crucial aspect of the company that had been left unquantified though and that was—what is the worth of TBK's brand equity? How valuable is the intangible brand? I reached out to a friend Aakanksha Gupta, who runs a leading PR firm called The Other Circle. I asked her, how does one measure brand equity or worth? Aakanksha suggested that we run an extensive market research campaign where we ask one thousand random people if they had heard about TBK. I didn't bite. It would take a lot of time and money and I had neither to spare. I asked myself, how can I show potential investors how much my brand is worth? I decided to take a straightforward approach and asked Aakanksha if we could simply calculate how much money any other business would have to spend to get the same kind of PR coverage that TBK got.

Whether it's magazine covers, international news and lifestyle channels, radio and even on reality shows, TBK has featured everywhere and we've not had to spend a rupee on any of it. We needed to drive that point home. Aakanksha sent me a table with a detailed break up of all the press and PR items I had shared with her against rack rates for centimetre footage in print publications, air time on TV and radio, and number of words on digital media platforms to arrive at a whopping (drum roll please) ₹6 CRORE. This number formed an integral part of my investor pitch and I spent a lot of time mulling over the figure we arrived at.

V Cats had regular day-long meetups with its network of investors to allow founders to present ideas to them. If any of these pitches caught their fancy, they could reach out to the founders and set up a one-on-one. It was a combination of *The Bachelor* and *Shark Tank*—finding the right match for founders and investors.

I had taken a fair share of meetings and felt a bit tired of the stiff, almost boring, way I was making these presentations. I decided I would try something different to make myself and TBK memorable in what was sure to be a parade of fantastic products, services and ideas. I decided to serve this lucky gathering of investors Mom's Smoked Mutton Kheema Samosas, hot off the tava. A quick call to V Cats and I learnt that the venue for the meetup did not have reheating equipment. I then called Mom, who suggested that I carry an electric fryer and have someone fry fresh samosas.

Woohoo!

I immediately called V Cats back to ask for permission. Quite unexpectedly, the lady on the line said, 'Yes, why not?' Before she hung up, she told me that most of the investors are vegetarian.

I didn't let this information dampen my spirits. We had some pretty outstanding Smoked Tur Dal Samosas, but I realized that high resolution, professionally shot photos of our Raan in Red Masala, Chicken Biryani and Chicken Cutlets dominated my presentation. I contemplated taking them out, but then decided not to overthink it and do what I do best with complete confidence—tell our story.

I always introduce myself to big audiences as the guy who quit Google to sell samosas. I think it does a spot-on job of telling people that (a) I was smart enough to get into Google and (b) I had enough conviction in my idea to quit Google. For the sake of my presentation, I had also developed a mission statement which I am quite proud of—to make Bohra food exciting for non-Bohras.

I elaborated on all of this and more in my presentation. I gave the investors a short history of the cuisine and community. I spoke about my mother and her rise to fame as head chef of TBK Home Dining Experiences. I presented product ideas and scale-up plans for delivery along with the concept of 'experience centres'. Then, we brought out the samosas. I organized lemon wedges to go with it along with little bowls of khajur chutney. For a few brief moments, everyone in the room was transported to the Kapadia home experiencing the first of our seven-course lunch menu. I told them exactly how to eat it and they did. And they reacted in the same way our guests do—they asked for more! What did I do? Request a cheque, of course.

Unfortunately, my pitch didn't always go down so well. I recall meeting a potential investor at the members-only Taj Chambers Suite situated inside The Taj Mahal Palace Hotel. While I had been to the Taj a few times before, I had never been to this ultra-exclusive meeting room of sorts. Compared to the meetings I was accustomed to having with vendors and staff in my tiny Worli kitchen, this was a massive upgrade. *Wow!* I thought to myself as I walked into the plush room. *I could get used to this.*

Mihir was stuck in a meeting and running late, so I began without him. I started with a short introduction of myself and TBK and then went on to elaborate on why I thought it would be a fantastic idea to invest in my business. After giving me a patient listening to, the investor politely asked me, 'Munaf, are you sure you want to do this? Once you raise funds, you will go down a path where everything you found entertaining, exciting and exhilarating about your little business might lose its charm. You will become accountable to others. It will be less about doing something to keep your mother busy and more about keeping your investors' funds busy. It will become less fun.'

I felt my confidence waver with that curve ball he had thrown. Then, I thought about what he was asking me. Did I really believe that raising money was what was required for the growth of the company? Was I victim to a trend or in it for the glamour or excitement?

Another investor told me that he wasn't really looking at the numbers, marketing and branding, or the capabilities of my team while evaluating TBK as an investment prospect. He was really just sizing me up, asking himself—can Munaf Kapadia deliver?

It's fascinating, but no equity investor will deny that start-ups have a high chance of failure. The only surety they want is that the founder will do everything s/he possibly can to avoid it. Time and again, I have been reminded that investors bank on the numbers, but they also bank on the founder—the human force behind it all who they need to trust and hold accountable. Your conviction, ability to handle tough questions and perform under pressure are some of the key traits that investors try and gauge over the several meetings and conversations that you have with them.

Looking outwards for help pushes you to look inwards and ask yourself hard questions like—do you really want to pursue this idea in the long term? Do you care about it enough to stick by your business in the wake of a crisis or fierce competition? Ask yourself these questions before you walk into a room because that self-awareness needs to reflect in your investor pitch.

I titled this chapter 'Raise Fun, Not Funds', because that is what I wish I did. I enjoyed certain parts of the journey immensely. Creating a pitch, learning about valuation, working with Mihir, etc., were very enriching experiences. The unnecessary stress I put upon myself was not. Navigating the labyrinth of questions and emotions that came as I met with investors was stressful, and the self-doubt that you develop can be debilitating. I'll never forget the first time I was told by an investor that he thought my valuation was highly inflated. I felt a rush of embarrassment; I almost wanted to apologize to him for my miscalculation. With time, and a few counselling sessions with Mihir, I got better at handling such remarks.

Fortunately for me, when the bids came in, we were oversubscribed at TBK. This allowed me to select investors whom I believed would add strategic and tactical value to my business. One of the first investors I brought on board was Rahul Akerkar, the renowned chef behind the Indigo chain of restaurants. While interested in the numbers, Rahul was keen to learn more about the food and my passion for the business. After I made my pitch, he said,

'Look Munaf, I'm in but I only make joint investments with another friend of mine.'

Rahul introduced me to the 'B' in the legal behemoth AZB & Partners. Bahram Vakil is one of the most well-respected and influential individuals I've ever had the privilege to meet, a man whose seniority in the legal field is only overshadowed by his humility. He and Rahul came on board as two of our first ten investors.

On 13 July 2017, I successfully raised ₹1 crore against a term sheet which stated that The Bohri Kitchen (now incorporated as Bohri Kitchen Pvt. Ltd.) is valued at ₹9 crore pre-money and ₹10.35 crore post-money. With a cap table any F&B entrepreneur would envy—Anirudh Damani of Artha India Ventures, Abhishek Agarwal of Rockstud Capital, Riyaaz Amlani, Rahul Akerkar, Bahram Vakil, Romil Ratra and Anup Deshmukh. I was optimistic about what the future held for TBK.

13

An Unforgettable Experience Centre

When I started operations in Worli back in 2016, I reluctantly considered allowing customers to pick up their orders from our delivery kitchen. I say reluctantly, because I wasn't very proud of the location or size of the space which was a matchbox located on the first floor of a crowded residential colony in the heart of South Mumbai. It was a complete antithesis to my home, where we hosted lavish dining experiences. Nonetheless, it was what I could afford at the time on my dwindling savings.

Weighing the demand, manpower and logistics costs of self pick-up against my embarrassment, I settled on a comfortable compromise. I fixed an alternate pick-up point close-by at City Bakery, Worli Naka. Customers were instructed to inform us once they reached the spot and one of the kitchen boys would then skip over to City Bakery with their order. I had strictly warned my team that under no circumstances were we to direct customers to the kitchen, even if we were short on staff. Also, to not keep customers waiting.

Despite my best efforts, one customer fell through the cracks. She had placed a very large order and the pick-up protocol had been communicated via WhatsApp, but for some reason she searched for directions to our location using Google maps instead of the link we had shared with her. It led her straight to our kitchen. She wasn't a first-time customer either—she had been home to eat and had ordered from our delivery outlet a couple of times.

When she called to tell me that she was downstairs, I panicked. Thankful that I was in the kitchen at the time, I yelled for one of the boys to rush and deliver her order. A few days later, this customer sent me a polite text to give me feedback on the food—which was excellent—and express her surprise at the location of our delivery kitchen. Although it was probably not her intent, I could sense disappointment in her tone.

I was desperate to move out of this delivery kitchen to a facility that was worthy of being shown off to customers, camera crews, collaborators and even friends and family. Fast forward to 2018, when I was flushed with capital from investors and could consider building my dream kitchen for the brand. Even before I signed the shareholder's agreement, I started the hunt for the perfect kitchen. I was driven by this strong feeling that, if I found the right kitchen, everything else would magically fall into place.

Considering how keen I was to move out of our existing location, the math I did to arrive at a budget for this grand project was juvenile at best. It went something like this—if I was paying ₹15,000 for two hundred square feet in Worli, then for a kitchen three times the size in the same locality, ₹45,000 was a reasonable budget. I contacted multiple brokers, friends in the industry and sent out messages[39] and emails to anyone who could help me in my quest.

At last, I had the capital, yet I set aside a paltry sum[40] for my rental budget. In the months and years to come, this proved to be a catastrophic decision. At the time, though, I was determined to do things as frugally as possible; for me, that was the underlying philosophy of doing good business. If I thought five times before spending my own money on the business, I needed to think at least ten times before spending a dime of investor money and rationalize every expense I made, no matter how big or small.

Home dining was by far our most exciting offering as a niche cuisine brand and any attempt at scaling the business felt incomplete without incorporating elements of the home dining experience into our growth model. This is what I had pitched to my investors as well. When I started viewing spaces for a new kitchen, I had a rough template for what I had in mind. My new central kitchen would feature a

---

39 Yup, the same famous WhatsApp broadcast or 'Dear Facebook' post I would normally reserve to brag about our latest achievement, this time around I used it to blast out a call for help—does anyone have a kitchen?

40 They say raising funds is hard. I say, spending funds is even harder. Especially for me, a first-time entrepreneur. I was just not in the habit of making quick financial decisions.

traditional thaal-style seating for ten to twelve people at the front of the house, while the rest of the space would operate as a delivery kitchen. The customer-facing section of the kitchen wouldn't function like a typical restaurant. Diners would have to reserve seats in advance, and we would only offer set thaal menus like we did in Colaba. I christened this all-in-one establishment TBK's Experience Centre.

Funny thing is, the only thing that proved to be experiential about this hybrid venture was the struggle I faced trying to set it up!

On the one hand, I had a specific vision in my head of what the space should look like. On the other hand, I had set a very small budget to fund it. My real estate brokers failed miserably in showing me anything that even remotely matched my specifications. I became so fed up that I'd jump on my Activa 125cc to recce the neighbourhood in Worli myself. Like a cop collecting information from his informers, I'd make enquiries with security guards or someone drinking chai on the street for details on rental properties and rates in the area.

After a week of making the rounds, all I had to show for it was a sore butt. Then, the first tranche of investor money hit the bank. I was officially on the clock now.

I continued to view kitchens that brokers showed me, widening my search beyond Worli. Eventually, I had no choice but to increase my budget[41].

---

41 I went from ₹45,000 to ₹50,000. It's only now that I realize had I doubled my budget, I might have spent an additional ₹12 lakh in a year but unlocked more than a crore worth of peace of mind.

A broker found a property in Worli (check), within my budget (check) and with a room that could potentially be transformed into an Experience Centre (or so I convinced myself). Having spent close to two months on this search, I caved; in doing so, I chose to overlook flaws in the interiors, construction and paperwork. If I was a traveller lost in a desert for weeks, this kitchen was a mirage that had been conjured by my mind. Under severe (and self-inflicted) pressure to move forward and minimize the opportunity cost for investors, I decided to settle.

If I thought my trials were over, well, the worst was yet to come.

Before signing the leave and licence agreement with the proprietor, my broker and I ran a due diligence on the title of the property. There was a discrepancy between the purchase deed and the title of the property, which had not yet been transferred from the previous owner's name.

That was the first red flag, but my broker and several other people I spoke[42] to assured me that this kind of waywardness was standard in commercial property dealings in Mumbai. Though unconvinced, I was persuaded by the feedback to go ahead and sign the agreement.

The lease was signed in November 2017. We were yet to move into the kitchen because requisite clearance for health, fire, etc., were to come through. I applied for our licences—Food Safety and Standards Authority of India

---

42 Another invaluable lesson in hindsight—there's such a thing as speaking to too many people!

(FSSAI), Health and the infamous Fire NOC—within the week.

Being a simple-minded and optimistic person, I assumed that I would be sending out orders for *New* Year's Eve deliveries from the *new* kitchen. I couldn't have anticipated that what was supposed to be, at the most, a month-long formality would turn into a three-month-long ordeal.

The time I had planned to invest in marketing my new kitchen, and generating and fulfilling orders, had to be rerouted into massaging the egos of government officials. I absolutely hated it. It was degrading, humiliating and, in the words of one of my advisers, a necessary wake-up call for what it takes to set up a F&B business in Mumbai.

NOC stands for No Objection Certificate, but I think it should be renamed NO Chance Certificate. For starters, I was unable to get a health licence (in the name of the landlord) because the property owner's name didn't appear on the title deeds. For two months, I chased the landlord to get the property transferred to his name. By the time he finally came around, a fire broke out at a popular bar in Kamala Mills. It was a tragedy that cost lives and injured many. This incident put the Brihanmumbai Municipal Corporation (BMC) on high alert with respect to granting Fire NOCs to food businesses. I bore the direct brunt of that. The official I had been corresponding with for my Fire NOC was placed on temporary leave in the days following the fire. I showed up every day at the BMC office for a week, pleading to get my application processed. The rules had changed overnight, and suddenly getting clearance wasn't ordinary compliance anymore.

Honestly, if I had just followed my instincts and ignored advice on the title deed from industry experts, I might have avoided this entire mess. Three months passed before I managed to get our paperwork through, and an inspection officer was appointed to examine our kitchen. It took all of twenty minutes. I finally had all the licences I needed to start business!

Work on the new kitchen had begun soon after I had signed the lease on the place. In fact, I got on the phone the very next day to speak to vendors about steel tables, fire systems, appliances, utensils, tools, etc. I spent the next week calling every person I knew who dealt in commercial kitchen equipment to understand costing, variety and logistics. I explored the option of buying second-hand equipment from friends and other business owners. In this jugaadu fashion, I bought steel tables, slotted angles, fancy cookware, deep freezers, storage units, etc., for a fraction of the retail cost. Kitchens that are closing host sales that are very similar to estate sales in the West. Equipment is auctioned off to the highest bidder and you get a moment's notice to show up and survey the goods. I had found equipment being given away practically for free; I ran strict quality checks to ensure that these were all safe purchases.

If I'm giving the impression that I was solely responsible for setting up this kitchen, please know that I, like Isaac Newton, was standing on the shoulders of giants.

One such giant was Bobby, owner of Crawford Market's iconic Sadanand restaurant by day and consultant on kitchen equipment by night. Bobby graciously drew out a blueprint of what my new kitchen should look like. He even advised me on the kitchen equipment I needed, how to acquire it, setting up infrastructure, etc.

And then there was my right-hand man—practically a family member now—Abdul Kadir Kayum.

A student at the Raheja Culinary Institute in Mumbai, Kadir had joined TBK to work part-time as a kitchen helper. Hailing from Bijapur, a small town in Karnataka where his father owns an ice factory, Kadir had a degree in mechanical engineering but his passion lay in cooking. His dream to become a chef led him to Mumbai—and by led, I mean he ran away from home!

Kadir's entrepreneurial bent of mind and genuine flair for food, especially Bohra food, led him to quit culinary school and join TBK full-time. He seamlessly facilitated our move between kitchens, allowing me to focus on finance, accounts and staffing while TBK continued to receive, produce and deliver orders[43]. It was a truly chaotic time and I don't know what I would have done without Kadir.

By mid January[44] in 2018, we had moved into TBK's new central kitchen. It was a big day for me and made my initial

---

43 We did a catering gig in Hyderabad for over five thousand people and Travelling Thaals for Hrithik and Farah during this period.

44 For someone who counted every penny I spent on my business in 2015–17 (since it was my meagre savings), these were anxiety-provoking times.

struggles seem worthwhile. We now had a state-of-the-art fire system, proper ventilation, double the water capacity of our last kitchen and enough room for preparation and storage. Not only had I upgraded to a bigger, swankier kitchen, but I also had a fantastic team in place and, for the very first time, a dedicated operations manager in Kadir.

While the kitchen was set up in record time, the ambitious Experience Centre remained a question mark. Setting up the kitchen cost a lot more than I had expected even though I had planned and anticipated expenses down to the last plug point. With the size of the kitchen, our sales target had also been tripled and we were looking at doing at least ₹18 lakh a month in business, with or without an Experience Centre.

Around this time, we began working with the Impresario team to set up our first-ever QSR at Flea Bazaar Café in Kamala Mills. Flea Bazaar Café was a concept food court comprising diverse cuisines and a bar. Riyaaz and his team had paid careful attention to the themes, menus, marketing and PR for every brand that had been given a stall. Each brand had a well-put-together personality, but TBK was perhaps the most outstanding of the lot. Our stall was made to resemble the old Bohra homes of Jamnagar (Gujarat), finished with tinted glass, a wooden facade and a little window through which orders were placed and served. They even got a mini thaal upon which the letters T-B-K were mounted.

While I wasn't investing in the CapEx through our recently acquired funds, I was acutely aware of the expenses that were going into putting up a simple QSR stall. My brand-conscious brain wanted this and a lot more for our own Experience Centre.

Our first-ever QSR at Flea Bazaar Café in Kamala Mills

Flea Bazaar Café launched in April 2018. A few weeks earlier, Kadir and I had a long and honest chat about the Experience Centre section of the kitchen. Even with funding, investing in it felt excessive since we had a customer-facing outlet at Flea Bazaar Café now. The Impresario team was willing to let me host thaal experiences at the QSR. It wouldn't be the ideal TBK dining experience—nothing close to the intimate meals that we hosted at home or what I had planned for the Experience Centre—but for now, it would do.

It turned out to be one of the smarter decisions I made about the business. I can't believe all the time I wasted trying to find a kitchen with a section suited for dining experiences. When I look back now, I'm amazed at how naive I was. How did I ever think that I could squeeze a dining area and delivery kitchen out of a space that measured six hundred square feet at a rental of ₹50,000 a month?

As for the area designated for the Experience Centre, we repurposed it to serve as Kadir's office and a call centre. Que sera sera.

FIRST, MAKE SURE EVERYONE WANTS TO BUY IT. THEN, MAKE SURE EVERYONE CAN BUY IT.

MAKE THE BRAND, STORY, PERSONALITY NICHE SO IT STANDS OUT FROM THE CLUTTER. MAKE THE PRODUCT MAINSTREAM SO YOUR BUSINESS IS SCALABLE.

14

When Mom Was Spotted Frying Samosas on an Air China Flight

I had barely gotten out of bed and fully gained consciousness. It was 23 November 2018[45], the morning after my birthday, and I had had a pretty busy night.

I opened my eyes to see Mom hovering above me.

'Now, how did you do this?'

'Do what?'

She gave me her phone. I exited the Candy Crush app and landed up on the family WhatsApp group which was abuzz with chatter about a video shared by my New York-based brother Mubbasir and his wife Sholeen who were on a flight back from Beijing. Imagine their shock when they

---

45 I was born on 22 November. Just like Bohra cuisine which has influences from both Yemen and Gujarat—I am both a Sagittarius and a Scorpio. It usually depends on the newspaper I chose to check the horoscope.

realized the inflight entertainment, with Chinese subtitles, was Mom standing at her kitchen stove, frying her signature samosas and explaining the recipe to celebrity chef John Torode. Luckily, they managed to record it.

This shoot had happened a while ago, when John and his crew had come home to sample a Bohra thaal while on an India food expedition. I had almost forgotten about it, but the video had somehow found its way to an Air China flight.

Imagine. A family based out of Colaba, Mumbai, decided to invite a couple of strangers to their house so they could share with the world the wonders of Bohra cuisine. And a few years later, it's on a TV screen inside an Air China flight. Mind Blown.

When it came to press and media coverage, TBK was an entrepreneurial dream. It was only when I was putting together a valuation of the company that I realized we had accrued coverage that, if paid, would have been worth ₹6 crore.

A question I would often get asked by friends and F&B peers was, 'Which PR agency do you have on board?' I would proudly tell them that I didn't have one. Since its inception in 2014 to this very day, I have spent almost nothing on press coverage[46] yet we have been featured

---

46 Okay, this is a half-truth. We have invested a lot in free samosas ☺

in the country's top news publications, radio, television and magazines.

The virality of the brand, and the interest TBK received, could be attributed to two broad factors. One, the inherently marketable and novel cuisine that is Bohra food. Two, the careful thought and patient relationship building that I had invested in for TBK to stay relevant and top of mind. My own painstaking positioning of the brand, and the many small tools and assets that I deployed to generate curiosity, has also been the part of our business that I have been most passionate about and had the most fun with.

When I break it down, there are three things that I committed to at the very beginning of my journey and continued to relentlessly devote time and energy to: (a) a damn good story (b) retelling that story at every opportunity I got and (c) continuing to build on the story over time.

Let me elaborate on this.

My friends and family are always taken aback at how easily I go up to celebrities in restaurants or at other social events, introduce myself as the Chief Eating Officer at TBK, give them my visiting card and invite them for a meal at our place. It's not above-average courage or confidence that allows me to do this, but the fact that almost every single time I've gone up to anyone, they almost always acknowledge that they've heard great things about TBK and would love to try it. Their response is usually something like, 'Oh, you're the guy who invites people home for lunch!' or 'You're the guy who started this restaurant with his mom,' or 'You used to work at Google and now you run a restaurant!'

Remember, to create a splash in a city with so much already happening, *you need to have a story worth telling.* TBK's origin story is not just about taking the Bohra thaal where no Bohra has gone before but it's also about a fight between mother and son over a TV remote. It's also about wanting Shah Rukh to come home for a meal. Imagine if Uncle Ben had never died in the Spider-Man origin story. If he had never told Peter Parker, 'With great power comes great responsibility.' While it's pretty cool that a radioactive spider bit Peter and made him Spider-Man, it's not enough. The story needs multiple arcs, each with its own purpose. Uncle Ben and Shah Rukh Khan/Television Remote are the emotional arcs that readers or foodies relate to.

My response to journalists would've been quite straightforward if I wasn't plagued by the need to tell stories. It would've been something like—I was inspired by the exquisite Bohra fare that I had grown up eating and saw vast potential in the cuisine and culture that had not found a footing in Mumbai's food scene. I was also extremely hell-bent on helping my mother find her life's purpose (the hero complex that I suffer from) and I saw great potential in her culinary skills.

Instead, I launched into a story about how Mom and I were fighting over the TV remote one afternoon and I told her quite arrogantly that I thought she needed to find better things to do with her time rather than watch saas-bahu shows. She gave me a good tongue-lashing, which forced me to think about what I could do to keep my incredibly talented mom busy.

All the above is true. I fought with Mom frequently over the TV remote. I was obsessively concerned with wanting to find something for her to do that went beyond her household responsibilities, a purpose, something that she looked forward to and was satisfying. These are normally the kind of interactions at home that we forget. It's so commonplace to have arguments with our moms over silly things like the TV or the menu for dinner but I chose to make it the cornerstone of our brand story. Something that everyone could relate to. It was something reporters found easy to write about and provided an angle that readers and viewers alike could relish!

I have gone so far as to give this kind of branding concept a name—I call it three-dimensional (3D) branding—where the product or service is the first dimension, the second is the visual identity (the actual logo, name, colours, tag line, mascot) and the third dimension is the emotion attached to the brand. The last can be brought out through faces, names of real people, the story (when and where it started, what it stands for and other intangible facets of the brand like its values)—all of which are woven into a storytelling and brand language that the founders choose to adopt.

My self-patented litmus test to check if a brand is 2D or 3D is to do a Google image search. See if the visuals on the first page mainly revolve around two dimensional aspects such as the logo, colours and products or are they deeper aspects such as the faces of the founders, their story, milestones, etc.

Over the years, TBK had grown enormously through digital storytelling. I used Facebook and then Instagram, WhatsApp, Google My Business and, eventually, a website (https://thebohrikitchen.com/) to engage my community of followers. I created a Zomato page for people to post reviews. TBK was not a restaurant and, at that point in time, we weren't even a delivery business. But I wanted reviews and ratings on a Zomato page because, for me, Zomato meant legitimacy.

I generated a lot of content around home dining experiences that featured the food, our guests, my parents and family members who played an important role in hosting and managing events. Mom and Dad created menus around seasonal ingredients, festivals and their moods, and I created events on Facebook so guests could make enquiries and bookings. The content on our Facebook page was so exciting that the press started picking things up from there and putting it in the paper without even telling me. (Not that I am complaining!)

I plotted a devious little system to ensure that we got as many conversations started around TBK on social media. I used to shamelessly bribe our weekend lunchers' with small jars of khajur chutney if they checked-in on TBK on Facebook. Not review or tag us, but check-in.

That's because my research told me that there was no better way of creating FOMO[47] amongst my target audience. When a friend of yours shows off that they've been to the most talked-about dining experience in the city and checks in, it feeds that desire to visit the place (and the address is masked! It just says Colaba). Also, it helped that our guests put up some amazing photographs and videos about their visit(s), tagging friends and urging them to do the same. It's no wonder we were sold out every weekend.

As I went along documenting our weekend events, our social media community kept growing slowly and steadily. Food is an easy subject to peddle on social media and the most surprising posts gained high traction with our followers. Look up 'Gheefication of the Lasan Kheema Bedu' on YouTube or Facebook. It's a thirty second-amateur video shot by me, of my mother putting generous amounts of ghee on an egg preparation we make during winters. It garnered eighty thousand views in just three days!

My WhatsApp database was exploding too. As bookings were always made via call or text (thanks to my No-Serial-Killer policy), my contact list grew larger. I tinkered with the idea of sharing WhatsApp updates with our patrons, but then my goal was to create FOMO. I told everyone that they had been enlisted into the 'Samosa Beta' List. This was marketed as an invite-only list of recipients, and only those who had made it for our home dining experiences

---

47 Fear of Missing Out

would qualify. They would get first-hand updates about upcoming events, new menu launches and maybe even free samples and invitations to brand collaborations. We were using it so effectively that the guys at WhatsApp even reached out to me to test WhatsApp for Business before it was launched for the public. Today, we have a dedicated number called the Samosa Helpline that sends out these WhatsApp messages to thousands of our 'Beta members'.

As exciting developments engulfed TBK, I made it a point to share the small and the big through social media. To me, it felt like TBK wasn't only about the service we were providing, it was also about my personal journey, along with that of my mother and my family. A natural outcome of this style of communication was that I saw tremendous engagement between our patrons and the brand. There are so many people who follow us on social media today who haven't ever eaten our food! For them, consuming our story was equally satiating.

When we were just starting out, I took every shred of interest anyone showed in TBK very seriously and for a long time, even after we had appeared on TV, print media and the radio, I said yes to every opportunity that came my way to address students, women entrepreneurs, start-up founders, home chefs and the like. No matter how big or small, I participated in a plethora of events where I could speak on a panel, give a talk or merely meet and have quality conversations with F&B entrepreneurs or young founders like myself. Being a 'yes man' in the early years of TBK helped me reap great rewards in the years that followed.

The hundreds of talks I've given—whether they were in other cities, colleges, corporates, founder-circles or even on a TEDx stage—I can only hope they were enlightening for the guests, but I can tell you they've all been incredibly inspiring for me. Meeting new people, witnessing how they are inspired by my story, that feeling of empowerment that if Munaf can do it, so can I. Those moments are very powerful for me. They give me purpose.

This book is being written with exactly that same objective. In a world where we're surrounded by stories of founders who raise billions for their unicorn start-ups, it can be very difficult to find an entrepreneurial journey which is equal parts aspirational but equal parts relatable.

I might not be a billionaire, but I know I've achieved enough to inspire you to get off your seat and maybe register that domain name you've been thinking about.

15

What It Means to Be Bohra

When I applied for the trademark for The Bohri Kitchen and TBK in 2015, my application was rejected by the registrar. 'Bohri is the name of a place and hence cannot be registered as a trademark,' he said. My lawyer patiently explained that we were not referring to the place (I didn't even know that Bohri was the name of a city/town!) but a cuisine that belongs to a community called Dawoodi Bohra. The registrar nodded slightly and said, 'Okay, but I still have to reject this. By your own admission, Bohri is a community. You can't trademark a community.'

My lawyer hesitated, but I stepped in. 'Sir, that's a common misconception. The community is actually called Dawoodi Bohra. We have intentionally been using the slang "Bohri" to avoid a complication exactly like this.'

Without wasting any time, I gently placed the *Forbes India* magazine which had my face on it before the registrar and clearly stated that I was Chief Eating Officer of The Bohri Kitchen. I also placed a box file which was filled with one hundred-plus newspaper clippings of all the press mentions we had received. And finally, I placed a jar of khajur chutney to highlight the extent and strength of the brand that he was refusing to register!

Not sure which one of these things did the trick, but he proceeded to award us the trademark for The Bohri Kitchen in long and short form!

Growing up, my Bohra identity was a distinction I always wore proudly. I was one among a handful of Bohra Muslims in my school. Even though my childhood was spent growing up in Byculla, a neighbourhood crowded with Bohra families, to me my family and relatives were the only Bohra folks I knew! As far as our religious education was concerned, we got one. Prayers, going to the mosque, fasting, etc., were things the adults in my life did and I participated when I absolutely had to. I preferred staying home and playing on my Sega console! Our academic performance was the only thing that my parents really cared about, and as long as we did well in that area of our lives (I didn't), my siblings and I were spared everything else. Mom and Dad made sure that we were a part of the community, but the extent of our participation was left up to us.

Being Bohra to me meant food—not just what we ate, but how we ate. As children and young adults, we frequently attended Bohra weddings and funerals with our parents. There was always the lure of catching up with distant relatives and cousins we hadn't met in a while but the one hundred per cent guarantee that there were would be a wholesome meal of some delicious Bohra food, prepared by one of the handful of Bohra bhatiyaras (caterers), at the end of all that socializing made me look forward to each and every one of these outings. Even at funerals, food remains an important part of the last rites performed as a tribute to the deceased. A simple but tasteful meal of Dal Gosht and Sau Danu is served along with some kind of dessert.

I savoured Bohra food as a child and later as an adult, and I loved being Bohra for it. Mom's fantastic cooking won me many friends at school, college and work. My Bohra-ness is rooted in our cuisine and I was happy to be the token Bohra in everyone's life taking Mom's home-cooked meals with me wherever I went.

At first, the TBK Home Dining Experience had very little to do with Bohra history, tradition and culture. It was about Mom's food and the preparation that went into Mom's food and, well, just the experience of eating Bohra food in a Bohra home!

I improvised my story with time to accommodate frequently asked questions by guests ranging from the extremely personal to the wildly political. The more personal questions included what I did, what my parents did, was I married, was I planning to get married anytime soon? Did I know so-and-so Bohra uncle or aunty? Where are these plates from? Are you religious? Is your Syedna (spiritual leader) pro-BJP? Do you think Saifee Hospital should keep their facade lights on all night? Are Bohras more, or less, conservative than Sunni Muslims? Why do you dress differently from the other Muslims?

I answered most of these questions with a non-committal nod or grin which indicated anything from Yes-Maybe-No! But where questions around the community were concerned, I felt it my responsibility to answer them as authentically as I could. After all, if I was the only Bohra person my guests ever had a conversation with, I wanted them to leave feeling a kinship with the community.

As TBK featured in the news and our social media following grew, Bohra men and women who were not known to us started following our pages and reaching out. All of them only had the most positive things to say. They felt proud that their food and culture was being talked about and adored by the media and guests alike. Being a small insular community, our achievements, culture, food, places of worship and thoughts on current affairs have always been kept within the community. Bohra food—which comes under the radar once every year during the month of Ramzan—had become a weekly affair because of TBK events.

We have hosted close to four thousand diners at TBK over the past five years and based on some very rough calculations, nine-tenth of them were non-Muslims. I'd like to think that food has, for long, been a bonding agent, a kind of voice that speaks to all people who choose to open their palates and themselves to it. It is an extension of culture and community that even an outsider can experience. It helps you forge connections with and appreciate a group of people that you may normally have no reason to really care about. When guests leave our house, they leave with a full belly and a full mind.

'Hi, can I speak to Munaf sir?' said what sounded like a young but confident student.

'Yes, speaking.'

'Sir, I would like to invite you to a Cafe@YSB event in Bandra as a keynote speaker.'

I remember being in the middle of something and hastily accepting the invitation without putting too much thought into it. I was expecting a small talk being organized by the local Rotary chapter or something equivalent at what I assumed was a café.

On the evening of the event, I found myself in front of what looked like a local mosque. A little nervously, I went up to the watchman and asked him if he had any idea what Cafe@YSB was? He told me to go inside the mosque. Suddenly, feeling incredibly conscious about my attire—in a Bohra mosque, the general attire is a kurta with a topi; I had come dressed for a casual talk at a coffee shop—I walked inside. Zahabia, my partner-in-crime for this event, was ready to bail. After all, women in a Bohra mosque are very much expected to cover themselves up in what we call a rida[48].

---

48 An Islamic modesty garment akin to the hijab.

'Listen, we've come all this way, my Spidey instincts tell me that this is going to be an interesting experience,' I said and somehow convinced her to stay.

And what an experience it was! Turns out that Cafe@ YSB was a youth initiative of the Khoja Muslim community, where they invite speakers to address the local community in their jamat-khanas (community centres). If it wasn't for the location, I would never have guessed this was a Muslim community event. It was very different from any Bohra Muslim gathering I had ever been to!

The kids led me to the stage and I thoroughly enjoyed addressing the community with my TBK experiences. I asked them to consider doing something similar within their own community. After all, Khoja Muslim cuisine is incredible as well! I've been trying to find a way to propagate a concept called TBK Chapters where we adopt one Bohra family across every city in the world (where they are located) and empower them to host at least one experience every month. It would be a great source of revenue for them and an incredible step in the right direction with my vision of making Bohra food famous.

This interaction with the Khoja community made me consider doing this with the larger Muslim community—I mean, as a Muslim myself, if I could be pleasantly surprised at how open and welcoming this community within Islam was, one can only imagine the potential to create awareness about the same amongst non-Muslims.

Not very long ago, I spoke at length with a potential investor about the opportunity for growth of a brand like

TBK that focused on a single cuisine. We were engaged in a back-and-forth when the investor in question suggested that perhaps marketing Muslim cuisine, or at least what is perceived as Muslim cuisine—meat, kebabs, Biryani, etc.—would face the backlash of the changing sentiment towards minority communities in the country. While this may not affect business directly in the short term, investor interest in such businesses might decline if, say, a campaign to #BanBiryanis gained traction.

As unlikely as that seems, I considered whether there is any basis for that line of thinking. I have always felt safe and comfortable with my minority status, never out of place, judged or discriminated against. That was in part my privilege. But tasked with a business to run that depended on the goodwill of people beyond my own circle of friends and family, I had to consider the possibility that what I was trying to do could also be seen as risky.

Still, it's hard to evaluate TBK's business prospects through a communal lens when you have seen what I have when running our home dining experience. The notional differences that exist in the minds of people are erased, or at least subdued, when they go beyond stereotypes and what we read in the news or hear from the mouths of elected public officials. It becomes that much harder to cultivate divisiveness and animosity when you *just know better*!

There is so much to be gained from a home dining experience apart from a good meal—it can foster goodwill, relatability and a richer understanding of communities that are different from our own. In fact, TBK has helped me realize what it means to be a Dawoodi Bohra myself.

YOU HAD THEM AT 'I'M AN ENTREPRENEUR'.

IT DOESN'T MATTER HOW WELL YOU SPEAK, WHAT YOU WEAR OR EVEN WHAT YOU'RE SELLING. YOU'VE WON THE CROWD WITH YOUR DECISION TO BECOME AN ENTREPRENEUR. NOW, JUST TELL THEM YOUR STORY.

16

How to Sell 200 Biryanis Per Day

Within a few months of moving operations to the new Worli kitchen in 2018, we were getting consistent feedback on the inconsistent quality of our food. So much for expecting a bigger, better kitchen to be a solution for all my operational challenges! As production levels doubled, we were also facing massive trials with inventory planning and managing wastage.

Kadir and a pair of ustads[49] who had been trained by Mom found themselves struggling to scale her recipes to meet the requirements of a commercial kitchen. It was clear that we needed an executive chef who had at least ten-plus years of experience in a commercial kitchen, to come on

---

49 Ustads are the 'Maharajs' of Muslim catering outfits. They may not be able to write recipes and create SOPs, but they are a treasure trove of family heirloom recipes and possess the magical ability to cook with andaaz. Just like Mom.

board and lead the production team at TBK. We now had the funding for it, and I was amazed that TBK had caught the interest of seasoned chefs, some of whom had worked in big restaurants and even five-star kitchens. Many of them came for the interview out of sheer curiosity.

'*Munaf, all of this started at home—with your mom—no way!*'

'*How did you get Riyaaz Amlani and Rahul Akerkar to put money in your venture?*'

'*You were on a reality show? And you won?!*'

'*Who handles your PR? You do it yourself? No way[50]!*'

Even as they would drill down for more information about how I had built my brand as a solopreneur, I was mining them for insights on setting up a scalable food delivery operation. These interviews helped me better understand how to set up a hub-and-spoke business model, the role of food partners in producing shelf-stable food, discounts, commissions, etc.

Through my network of advisers, chefs and friends in F&B, I learnt everything I could about on-demand, scalable food delivery. Simultaneously, I modelled and implemented food production and supply networks on the operational templates of what some of the biggest and most successful delivery chains in the country were using. I immersed myself in fine details—unit economics, organizational hierarchies, size of their kitchens and even their food

---

50 There was one candidate who said 'no way' a lot.

partners as they went about creating five-kilometre bubbles and populating each city with thirty-plus kitchens.

I absorbed this information like a sponge and made one startling discovery. Pioneers like Dominos and Rebel Foods had already mastered food delivery; I simply had to learn from them. While Ranveer Brar taught me how TBK was much like a bicycle, the prospective chefs that I met showed me that I didn't have to reinvent the wheel to ride it!

Interestingly, I realized that there was one major difference between these players and TBK. They were either multi-brand (Rebel Foods owns Behrouz Biryani, Oven Story, Faasos, etc.) and/or multi-cuisine outfits (Fresh Menu sells Chinese, European and Indian food). TBK was a single-brand-single-cuisine concept.

I also learnt that the highest-selling brand in these kitchens did an average monthly business of ₹5-6 lakh, which meant I had to keep my overheads and CapEx low to turn profitable quickly.

In my original pitch for round one funding in 2016, my TBK scale-up plan consisted of outlets which would be part delivery and part walk-in experience centres. It's only post-funding, while learning on the job, that I realized food delivery is a very different specialized beast that requires a focused operational strategy if you are to have profitable unit economics. For an outlet to break even at ₹5-6 lakh your entire profit and loss statement needs to be designed from ground up. Rentals need to be kept below five to seven per cent of target revenue, CapEx needs to be at such a low level that you can recover it from the profits generated in six months. This information formed the foundation of my ultra-light distribution model. As a single brand, aiming to have twenty-plus delivery kitchens in Mumbai, I shouldn't expect more than ₹6 lakh in sales per month per outlet.

With all this at the back of my mind, I launched my third kitchen in January 2019. I used this kitchen, which I set up in collaboration with OYO Rooms in a Juhu hotel, to test my new plan to set up ultra-light kitchens which would be profitable within four months of going live.

I had learnt a lot from my experience of setting up the new Worli kitchen and, even if I wasn't wiser, I definitely wasn't going to be as foolish as I was the last time around. Based on my research, I devised five golden rules for building this new scalable delivery model.

#1: Outsource eighty per cent of your menu

This was by far one of the hardest things for me to embrace. There was no concept of maximizing profits at TBK. The business was built on the idea of sharing a slow-cooked, home dining experience with guests.

The same approach, when applied to delivery, did not work. The lack of standardization in our menu meant delivery customers, who had come to expect a particular flavour or a certain level of generosity in our portions, were disappointed.

I realized that customer expectation from home dining was very different from home delivery. A home dining (or Travelling Thaal) customer wanted a seven-course highly experiential meal and had no qualms about paying ₹1,500 (per person) for it. A TBK delivery customer, on the other hand, was looking for an ₹250 box of Bohri Dum Biryani or six Smoked Mutton Kheema Samosas available within the hour and tasting the same *every single time.* Clearly, each model warranted a completely different operational DNA.

Additionally, the unit economics were a game changer. Consider the per sale cost break-up:

Aggregator 20 per cent
Food & packaging 40–45 per cent
Promotions & discounts 10–20 per cent
Total earning 10 per cent

Add cost of wastage, you would have barely broken even!

The solution for consistency and increased shelf-life was to work with food partners. It wasn't easy to convince players who supplied the Starbucks and McDonald's of the world to entertain a brand with barely twenty orders per day, but I got lucky.

We spent a lot of time standardizing Mom's recipes, with the combined expertise of Chef Rahul Akerkar, friend and consultant Devansh Jhaveri, Kadir and the food scientists employed by our food partners. By the sixth blind tasting, I could identify Nafisa Kapadia's Biryani just by the aroma. It took over two months for us to work our way through Mom's recipes and make them commercially viable. To keep our IP (intellectual property) rights intact, we signed an airtight NDA (non-disclosure agreement) with our partners and made the masalas in-house and supplied them to the food factories.

In 2016, when I started the delivery kitchen, I struggled to make more than a few kilos of Biryani every day and deliver it beyond a five-kilometre radius from Worli. By the end of 2018, my food partners and I had successfully created a supply chain capable of making one thousand-plus boxes of Biryani per day, available for next-day delivery at any one of our kitchens in Mumbai or Pune (which was part of my expansion plans). Plans to make it available pan-India were in the pipeline.

#2: No fire in the kitchen

Almost half the struggle to begin operations from our new Worli kitchen had to do with getting permission for a gas bank system from the authorities. This came in the form of a fire licence, followed by a health licence.

Understandably, there are strict eligibility guidelines to follow in order to get an open-flame fire NOC. For example, your kitchen must have a back door. Getting an affordable space in Mumbai is hard enough; finding a space with a back door as part of the original building plan is next to impossible!

My research revealed that almost all the large food delivery operations use induction stoves, combi ovens or microwaves instead of kitchen burners. Their entire back-end supply chain is optimized to ensure they only have to assemble and reheat food, prepared by food partners, in their outlet kitchens. This is called the hub-and-spoke model.

Once I wrapped my head around this, things started to fall into place. I immediately saw the benefits—my broker, for one, began showing me so many more affordable properties I never had access to before! The additional expense of kitchen equipment and electricity could be justified by the overall scalability of this model. Now we could explore real estate as affordable as ₹100 per square foot.

#3: No cash inside the kitchen

Towards the end of 2016—around the time that I discovered I was bankrupt—I caught one of my employees stealing from the cash box. Cash on delivery (COD) was a large percentage of our sale, but it was a challenge to collect cash daily from the kitchen. As my ambition grew beyond a couple of outlets, I needed a system for cash management.

My relationship manager at HDFC Bank gave me a great (albeit slightly expensive) solution. For ₹8,000 per month, per outlet, they would send a bank representative to collect cash daily from each of our outlets and deposit it into our account.

#4: No orders via calls in the kitchen

Almost a year into running our delivery business, I continued to answer calls for enquiries and orders. I genuinely enjoyed interacting with customers, but as our orders per day went up, it became impossible for me to do it.

With a sales target of ₹6-7 lakh per kitchen, I couldn't find the budget to hire an English-speaking phone operator. The role then transitioned to the kitchen helpers. While the helpers were trained to be exceptionally polite, they really couldn't do anything about the noise in the kitchen. It's no surprise, then, that mistakes were made while taking down the orders.

We've had everyone from Deepika Padukone to politicians randomly calling the kitchen for Biryani. So once funding came in, I invested in a dedicated resource to handle calls—a charming, English-speaking customer care executive who worked out of our head office at Churchgate. A centrally managed lead management system was used to relay orders to each kitchen based on the customer's address.

#5: Keep CapEx <₹5L and Rent < ₹25K

I had painstakingly worked backwards from the ₹6 lakh sales target to calculate that the model only worked if I kept my fixed costs to a minimum. So my last, but most important, rule for a TBK delivery kitchen was to keep CapEx under ₹5 lakh and rent under ₹25,000.

With a lot of help from different suppliers, relentless negotiating and careful purchase of both first and second-hand items, we put together an equipment list which became our go-to shopping manual for the new delivery kitchens. We further optimized our operational SOPs to ensure that this equipment fit within a 250 square feet space, leaving enough room for four kitchen helpers and two kitchen managers to comfortably cater to ₹6 lakh worth of delivery orders.

By the end of August 2019, we had a total of five delivery kitchens for TBK in Mumbai—Worli, Kamala Mills, Khar, Juhu and Lokhandwala. We managed an average of two hundred orders per day, impressive when you consider Khar and Lokhandwala were new kitchens, and that in 2016 we were doing 20-25 orders on an average.

While my golden rules gave me clarity and the ability to make faster decisions, execution was only possible because of the fantastic team I had in place by then.

It began with the original team—Mom, Dad, Monu and Anjum—who had been managing the home dining experiences since 2015.

By mid 2017, Kadir had joined us as a kitchen helper so he could learn from the ground up; very quickly, he started managing TBK's operations. Rizwan Amlani, founder of DOPE Coffee and Riyaaz's brother, gave Kadir some great advice. 'If you want to grow in your career, Kads,' he said, 'make Munaf feel like he has no work, at least with regards to operations, because you're taking care of everything in the background. This will make you indispensable.' Kadir took that advice to heart and worked his way up at TBK. He even bought a stake in the company when I raised funds in 2018. In June 2019, when we had our very first TBK town hall, it was Kadir who acted as host and acknowledged the efforts of our leadership team.

When Kadir took on the role of head of production, working with our food partners to scale Mom's recipes, Milind Mutke joined us as Operations head. With over ten years in the F&B industry, he had considerable experience in setting up kitchens and played a pivotal role in implementing the above strategy.

It's surprisingly difficult to find someone who can make sense of the myriad sources of revenue and expenses in a food business and ensure you are being paid what you are owed. I hired, and unfortunately had to fire, more than three accountants prior to the talented Manisha Bhoir, who joined us as senior accountant.

Mercifully, my then fiancée (now wife!) Zahabia took on the marketing for TBK and was pivotal to us going from ₹6 lakh per month in 2017 to ₹35 lakh in August 2019. She led Mariyam Kachwala and Pankaj Vishwakarma, who handled social media and aggregators respectively. Mandar, Jigna and Trevor at the head office looked after administration and handled the call centre.

June 2019: TBK's very first town hall.

In June 2019, when this photo was taken two months prior to our highest sales numbers, our team strength was over forty people. I remember when I walked into the banquet hall in PVM Gymkhana that we had booked for the town hall, I was completely taken aback by the sheer size of my team. The last time I had been to an office function with so many people in one room was the Google Mumbai office Christmas party. A full circle.

I was proud of myself that day. I remember thinking that while TBK still didn't pay me enough and neither did delivering two hundred Biryanis do anything to solve global warming, my efforts had created employment for over forty people. It was an incredibly powerful feeling and sharing that moment with my parents, who were the chief guests that day, meant everything.

From 2015 to 2019, it felt like a lifetime but clearly, this was just the beginning. I wanted to make Bohra food famous and build a brand that the world would sit up and take note of. I could do that by enabling a grand network of Bohra families to conduct their own TBK Dining Experience across the globe. I could focus on our flourishing catering business (aka the Travelling Thaal). I could package and sell ready-to-eat frozen samosas or jars of khajur chutney to supermarkets. I called this my grand omni-channel vision for TBK.

But first, I had to take our food delivery ambitions to a logical level of scale and sustainability.

17

I Don't Need Google, Mom Knows Everything

To see Mom hovering over gargantuan vessels in the sweltering heat of our home kitchen, dipping into pots and pans swiftly for a quick taste of this and that, prepping the next batch of ingredients even as she snatches quick peeks at her phone, you would think she was a born culinarian. Hard to believe that, as a girl, she had never set foot in the kitchen except to serve herself a meal!

One evening, when Mom and I had been running TBK's Home Dining Experiences for almost two years, we sat down together to go over questions for an interview that she had to give in her role as head chef[51]. As we went down the list, reading question upon question about what it was like working with her son, cooking for her family, cooking for strangers, being famous, etc., I realized I had never bothered asking her these questions myself. I had once read

---

51 Even though Mom was very much the head chef of TBK, we lovingly called her the 'Mom Chef'.

something on the internet that really stuck with me—who were our mothers, before they became our mothers? I had been wondering for some time now, was she truly happy operating TBK or had I foisted my own ambitions upon her? So, I took this opportunity to ask her:

'Mom, when you were younger, what did you want to do with your life?'

Nafisa Kapadia né Masalawala was an only child raised by doting parents in a simple, middle-class home in Mumbai's Bohra Mohalla[52]. She excelled at school and was surrounded by adoring friends, many of whom she continues to be in touch with till date.

Growing up, Mom aspired to be financially independent. She told me, in response to my question, that as a young person she aspired to be a career woman. Her parents encouraged her to study and pursue a higher education with the intention of allowing her to work and build a career for herself. While I am certain that marriage was not far from their minds, my grandparents chose not to make that a priority for her. After completing her BSc in chemistry and botany, she took up a secretarial studies course so that she

---

52 This part of South Mumbai is home to perhaps the city's largest Bohra neighbourhood with all kinds of establishments run or occupied by Bohra families. As I write this, the mohalla of Mom's childhood has ceased to exist, with the older, squat buildings being razed to make way for towers, complexes and malls.

could work with a corporation, a coveted career track even then. She also completed a short home science course, as was customary in those times, for instruction on how to run her own home.

She secured the first job she applied for and embarked on a career as secretary to the Swedish General Consul in India.

By age twenty-five, when Mom was personal assistant to the chief marketing officer of Indian Data Management, her professional life came to a grinding halt. She got engaged to my father and, from what she tells me, she quit work immediately because that was considered the respectable thing to do once you got married. After marriage, there was still hope that she might re-enter the workforce but it wasn't a priority by any means.

Mom's mother, my nanima, was a fantastic cook. Mom only entered the kitchen after she got married and my dadi, her mother-in-law, was a task master who kept all the women of the house on their toes. Between raising her four children, undertaking responsibilities to run our large household and managing her mother-in-law, it seemed unlikely that Mom would go back to a conventional nine-to-five desk job.

But being the enterprising woman that she is, Mom continued to learn from and embrace the challenges that were thrown her way with aplomb. One of them was cooking. She was trained by Dadi, a personality who was no less demanding than a Michelin-starred chef. My dadi's complete management of the kitchen at home ensured that only the best ingredients were acquired to prepare meals, and even simple food made for daily consumption was cooked strictly as per recipe. Her meticulous standards have trickled down and shaped the way we host our home dining experiences today.

As my siblings and I got busy with school, Mom began to explore small business opportunities, things she could do from home that would keep her busy and help her earn a small steady income. She ventured into crochet, crafting household items that she could retail to neighbours, family members and friends. She made and sold chocolates, and became an Amway representative, but none of these initiatives fuelled her creative side or passion for work. Today, when I ask her why nothing really stuck, she says, 'Business just isn't for me.'

Had she given me this response prior to us setting up TBK, I might have agreed with her. Mom is essentially a homebody. She thrives with a routine. Her commitment to her family has been unwavering through the years and she genuinely enjoys caring for us and attending to our needs. But after working with her for almost five years as co-founder and business partner of TBK, it was obvious that Mom is cut out for so much more.

Listening to Mom talk about her aspirations as a young woman, I couldn't help but think about the immense privilege I enjoy in being able to choose who I want to be or what passions I want to pursue. Even though Mom never lets on, I am certain that she must have pined for at least some part of the ambition that she traded to have a family.

Even before TBK was conceived, I had the nagging conviction that Mom had the potential to excel at anything she put her mind to and that often left me with overwhelming feelings of guilt. I wondered if we hadn't done enough as a family to help her realize her personal goals.

My parents' motto has been to educate us and then leave us to our own devices.

The first-ever lunch we hosted as The Bohri Kitchen took Mom by complete surprise. She didn't expect or imagine the kind of appreciation that we received from our diners. Soon, Mom and Dad were leading the operations of the project and as a team, my parents are like two excited kids when it comes to food. From Biryani lunches for their kids to Sheer Kurma for Eid, they love sending people treats. I recall their heated debates about the weekend lunch menus that went on late into the evening, after Dad got back from a full day of work at his shop. At times, the discussion would continue for two days as they plotted how they would treat guests to dishes that they had never eaten before. Then, a few days prior to the event, a similar discussion would ensue around purchase. What if item X wasn't available in Y quantity or what if it wasn't fresh? Should the menu be tweaked, should we make a smaller portion or use a different ingredient in its place? My head would spin listening to their contingency plans. Those were the early days, though. Eventually, the system became foolproof. My parents could practically dream up menus and delegate shopping, if need be.

I always knew she was an enterprising woman, but I never expected Mom to adapt so quickly to the new challenges I kept throwing at her. At age sixty, she brings an ease to the chaos that reigns in the kitchen. She gets hot and tired but never irritable or hassled.

One of my tasks was to screen callers before confirming their bookings. As enquiries multiplied, I asked Mom if she'd run my No-Serial-Killer policy check on potential guests. I thought she would refuse —after all, she was managing the entire operations more or less on her own—but, surprisingly, she didn't. In fact, she smoothly transitioned into the role of what I—quite ingeniously, I believe— called the voice of TBK, answering calls, screening guests, responding to Facebook messages and enquiries on WhatsApp.

Turns out Mom is fantastic at generating business. Having the chef behind the famous brand answer the call definitely had a positive impact on customers, and Mom's ability to spontaneously give potential customers not-on-the-menu options and recommendations further benefitted conversion rates. Every once in a while, I would notice additional items being served at lunch or dinner simply because Mom had been coaxed into adding an extra course or two! And at the same price per head. Of course, she couldn't refuse. I'd ask her to not indulge these requests, but soon learnt that my disapproval had no impact on the way she chose to conduct business. TBK's Zomato and Google reviews spoke in glowing terms of the hospitality extended by my parents. In the eyes of all our home dining guests, Mom was a celebrity. The acknowledgement and recognition she received led her to take better care of herself.

For almost two years, Mom had been putting off a critical knee replacement surgery which had severely compromised the quality of her life. Her ability to step out of the house was also restricted because our old building doesn't have a lift. It's not like she was afraid of surgery or the months of recuperation that would follow, but I think she had convinced herself that she simply didn't need it. Working on a project she cared about and excelled at, especially a physically demanding one like TBK, changed her outlook on this, or at least that's what I like to believe. In August 2016, Mom finally agreed to have her knees operated upon. It was the first time she was being hospitalized and we were all aware of the long duration of post-operative care that was essential for a complete recovery. Our sombre mood got a much-needed lift when we discovered the BBC video that we had shot for TBK almost a year ago was ready to air. We watched the whole thing together, on the TV in her hospital room!

After the first couple of years of hosting home dining experiences, Mom confessed that as elated as she was at the response, she had never expected TBK to gain legitimacy as a business. She assumed that I would get bored of running this on the 'side' or become so overwhelmed trying to juggle these at-home pop-ups and work that my enthusiasm would eventually die down.

When I put in my papers at Google, I came home and informed my parents as stoically as I could that I had finally resigned. They were immensely disappointed.

Mom wasn't very vocal about how she felt at the time, but she supported Dad's point of view. She kept her feelings from me then, perhaps because Dad was already voicing his concerns and displeasure voraciously enough. Months after I left my job, she told me how torn she had been about my decision to leave a lucrative, thriving career at a prestigious company for what was essentially a mom-and-pop-shop operation being run from home. She was more worried than upset, thinking about what my future would hold if my attempt at entrepreneurship failed. Mom knew that, unlike my siblings who had found their passions, I was still lost where my career was concerned.

Over the next year and a half, Mom found herself arbitrating heated arguments between Dad and me on the subject of how TBK should be run. It was almost funny how these conversations would usually begin with something small, like the selling price of our samosas, and inevitably turn to my unwitting decision to quit Google!

Looking back, though, I can only imagine how painful that period might have been for Mom. Growing up, I was extremely attached to her. Being the youngest among four children meant that a lot of her attention was focused on my needs. I would emotionally blackmail her to get whatever I wanted. When she picked me up from school, I'd badger her until she bought me a McDonald's soft serve. When we went shopping, I pestered her endlessly to buy me video games. On weekends, I'd insist she make my favourite food. She would acquiesce, even if only because she was just completely sick and tired of my nagging. It was Mom who I always turned to when I faced challenges at school and college—be it my discomfort with the socio-economic disparity between my peers and me or the embarrassment I experienced at the onset of aggressive teenage acne.

Over the last five years of being CEO of TBK, personally and professionally, I have grown by leaps and bounds. Mom, who has won awards and achieved semi-celebrity status with a growing list of fans in Bollywood (serenaded by Shaan on her birthday!), food and politics, hasn't changed one bit.

Today, when I look at Mom, she seems as content and satisfied with her life as she's always been. I'd like to think that TBK has done something for her too. I hope it gave her a sense of fulfilment and joy. I hope it made her look forward to her days in a way that only having a purpose or being brilliant at doing something makes you.

The greatest irony of all is that the world believes that TBK was born out of a son's desire to help his mother realize her dreams. While it may have started out that way, it really became about my mother helping me realize my own. Yet again.

Mom and I have always been very close (Photo courtesy Hindustan Times).

THE DIFFERENCE
BETWEEN A
MILLION DOLLARS
AND ONE CRORE IS
PEACE OF MIND.

RAISING FUNDS IS A
FULL-TIME JOB, IT'S
NOT SOMETHING YOU CAN
DO WHILE BUILDING A
FOUNDATION FOR YOUR
BUSINESS. SO, RAISE
ENOUGH SO THAT YOU'RE
NOT CONSTANTLY IN THE
FUNDING RACE.

18

My Plan to Save the World with Home Dining Experiences

Writing formulas is my thing. While working on The Dining Table, I gave some thought as to why TBK had been elevated to celebrity status.

My formula went something like this:

HOME DINING EXPERIENCE = FOOD (Home Chef + Authentic Delicious Cuisine) + EXPERIENCE (Home + Story of the Community and the Family)

According to my equation, the success of a home dining event is based on two factors. Half its success, in my opinion, depends on creation of a genuine experience for guests. Obviously, the food is critical but our story—a mother with an outstanding repertoire of heritage recipes partnering with her son who works at (and later quit) Google—is central to the TBK experience. As is the fact that we offer an authentic Bohra cultural experience, with food curated by a Bohra home chef and hosted at our Bohra-themed-and-styled home.

Today, a growing number of people are keen to learn about, appreciate and dine on food and drink that reflects a culture outside of their own. What these diners are looking for is a cross between a trip to a museum or gallery and dining at an ethnic food restaurant.

My home in Colaba, Mumbai, is ideal for anyone wanting to immerse themselves in Bohra culture. The two-storey building is over seventy years old, and everything—from the choice of green-and-white marble floor tiles and light wood panelling in our living room to the tall photo of the Kaaba in Mecca and choice of upholstery—lends an old-world Bohra charm to my home. The menu, comprising Mom's recipes and menus revised every week, stays as true to Bohra practices as possible. We take our guests through a lot of history and entertaining facts around our culture and cuisine. Dad serves and dotes on guests personally; when you've had your fill of samosas or Biryani and you say, 'I'm done', all he's hearing is, 'I want more!' All of this comes together beautifully to elevate a simple lunch or dinner to the status of being an activity. At the end of which you've learnt something and participated in age-old customs and traditions that you wouldn't have the chance to otherwise. It's the definition of doing something 'different' in the city on a Sunday afternoon.

Though I raised investment to start my delivery business, I had yet to find a way to scale home dining experiences. My initial idea to create The Dining Table app didn't see the light of day. However, I believe with all my heart that there is an opportunity here. Around the same time that TBK was growing in popularity, other incredibly talented home chefs were also promoting regional cuisines—Perzen Patel who started The Bawi Bride, Alefiya Jane for East Indian food or Kalpana Talpade for Pathare Prabhu cuisine. Today, thanks to all the innovative work being done by entrepreneurs across mainstream and niche cuisines and concepts like home dining, catering, delivery, cooking tutorials, etc., home chefs have a voice in the vast, competitive and fast-evolving F&B forum. The notion that TBK is a seasonal venture or pop-up run by a home chef and the regular misconceptions that plague small food businesses have once and for all been banished.

Two things became clear. One, there are talented home chefs who are keen to showcase their culinary talent through home dining experiences. Two, there is a customer genuinely open to new cuisine and willing to spend on it. What was the best way to connect them?

In 2018, I had a chance meeting with Keya Khanvte, entrepreneur and proprietor of a boutique travel company. We bumped into each other at a food festival in Mumbai where she and her eight-year-old son were doing the rounds.

Keya had travelled widely across the state of Maharashtra and her consultancy work in tourism development gave her insight into how home dining experiences could be shaped into a valuable tourism asset for the state and country. Both of us felt passionately about stretching the boundaries for what the city had to offer tourists and travellers. We spoke briefly at this event; weeks later, we reconnected and spoke extensively over the next few months on Maharashtra's potential for experiential tourism.

Up until I met Keya, I looked at home dining experiences through the lens of empowering home chefs. I was exploring the private sector approach to enhancing and expanding the concept. With Keya, I was able to broaden that lens and explore the possibility of enlisting public stakeholders in scaling home dining experiences as a concept.

We spent a good two months ideating on the culinary potential of the state of Maharashtra.

Mumbai is the top tourist destination in India. Not just for foreigners, but also domestic travellers who visit the city for business and pleasure. Mumbai has the tourism potential of a world-class city. The city is a convenient access point to the rest of the country because of which even if Mumbai isn't the destination of choice, it acts as a port of entry. Add to that moderate to high temperatures all year round, colonial architecture, the sea and cheap food, drinks and shopping. Tourist traffic is inevitable, yet the city's infrastructure and public services don't account for tourism in any way. Disparate agencies, hotels and companies have formed a network of tourism support services—tours, guides, day trips and a host of other activities basis which the existing tourism business is still surviving. Despite this effort, one aspect of the tourist experience is grossly under-promoted by the government and allied bodies and that is food.

I spent some time looking up websites dedicated to tourism in popular destinations. I spoke to friends I knew in the tourism industry and even carried out a simple primary research among family friends on what they did to entertain out-of-towners in the city. Food was coming up as the top response from all quarters. As resident Mumbaikars, we often took for granted the wide variety of domestic and global cuisines we had access to and for all budget sizes. A good meal constituted everyone's idea of culture and entertainment. The city is jam-packed with restaurants serving popular international cuisines and Indian fare. But none of these offer the experiential charm of a home dining experience that combines food with history, personalized service and a human connection.

The intimacy of home dining experiences is unparalleled in the F&B industry, something that tourists, travellers and expats crave in foreign cities. It is also a concept that Airbnb experiences was trying to compensate for by creating a separate business vertical under their existing brand to allow locals to offer one-of-a-kind experiences to travellers.

The more Keya and I brainstormed together, we grew increasingly confident that home dining experiences would be a phenomenal tourism asset and could shape India into a destination for all kinds of experiential dining opportunities. The rationale behind approaching Maharashtra Tourism Development Corporation

(MTDC) was to assist us with outreach. We needed funding to identify and activate the home chef networks in Maharashtra and the resources to market home dining experiences to tourists and tourism departments abroad.

Keya was due to make a presentation to Maharashtra Chief Minister Devendra Fadnavis at the time on how to improve inbound tourism in the state. She made a spontaneous decision to make home dining experiences part of her recommendations. Eventually, when she made the presentation to Mr Fadnavis, he made special note of home dining experiences and asked her to approach Mr VK Gautam, Principal Secretary of the Tourism and Cultural Affairs Department, to take the project ahead with the government.

To this end, we drew up plans in the form of a pitch deck that would sufficiently satisfy the officials in the Maharashtra Tourism department to endorse the home chef industry. Both Keya and I agreed that in order to execute our vision, we would need a team in place to focus on business development, marketing and research. For this we needed funding from a major stakeholder in the enterprise—the state government.

Many meetings took place between me and Mr VK Gautam before I invited him home for a meal one evening. Mom's food did what I couldn't do with elaborate presentations, statistics and photographs. Mr Gautam has become the self-appointed evangelist for home dining experiences. As our conversations with him advanced, he expressed genuine support for our initiative and provided invaluable guidance in ensuring our proposal reached the right stakeholders in the government.

Keya and I put together two broad proposals for the home dining agenda. The first version sought direct government funding and the second one made a specific pitch for marketing support. To me, personally, home dining experiences was a project. I didn't see myself expending any more bandwidth than I already was. I emphasized the need to create teams and acquire a good database of home chefs and a directory of regional cuisines that were available in Maharashtra. I was most proud of the marketing plan I had put together. Everything that I had ever done for TBK was laid out on those slides in a focused and step-by-step format.

In the proposal where we sought enlistment in the tourism budget for the state, we specifically requested (a) use of ad inventory through online and offline channels, (b) access to travel agents affiliated with the Maharashtra government, (c) opportunity to address industry conferences and forums to promote home dining, (d) funding home chefs to represent Indian cuisine on international platforms, be part of larger tourism campaigns, collaborations with airlines, etc.

Soon enough, we refined what we were bringing to the table (quite literally!) and what we would need from the government to unlock the revenues that home dining experiences were sure to bring. Mr VK Gautam helped us secure a brief meeting with Mr Jaykumar Rawal, then Minister of Tourism, to present our case. I was promised not more than five minutes with the gentleman but ended up spending forty minutes taking him through the road map for making Maharashtra the model state in promoting home dining experiences. Mr Raval asked detailed questions on every aspect of the proposal and heard us out patiently. I had to keep reminding myself that this was a man who spoke to ten people like me every single day and I should be wary of *eating* into my pre-assigned time. I demonstrated no restraint despite this. Before the meeting ended—and what came as a complete surprise to me— Mr Raval conclusively advised us that requesting a grant would be a tedious, long-drawn-out affair, but provisional marketing aid would come to us sooner. He advised me not to ask the government for investment per se, but to ask for their support in promoting and marketing the concept effectively instead.

These few key interactions with the Maharashtra Tourism department resulted in an invitation from MTDC to speak on a panel on World Tourism Day. The panel comprised of speakers from different sectors of the tourism industry to present the innovation they were bringing to hospitality management, F&B and transport. My short address focused on our journey of running TBK and the vast opportunity that existed in this micro-category of tourism that, if developed properly, could reap millions in revenue for the Indian economy. It was a proud moment for me. My parents, then fiancée (now wife) and future father-in-law were present for my presentation to the minister, as were eminent officials from the tourism department. It felt good to be able to give voice to my ambitions for home dining experiences.

With some gentle pestering from my end, we even put together a tourism task force comprising Riyaaz Amlani, Farah Khan, Gogi Singh, Romil Ratra, Keya, VK Gautam and me.

When working with the government, one critical attribute is patience. Governments will change, bureaucrats too, but you have to find a way to stay on their radar with an eye on that ultimate prize, to scale home dining experiences with the help of the government. I'm hoping that by the time this book is published I would have closed a formal arrangement with the Maharashtra Tourism department to bring me on board as a consultant to help them propagate home dining experiences!

Irrespective of whether this happens in the next few months or next few years, for me it's worth the wait. I'm convinced that home dining experiences can save the world. We unfortunately live in a time where, instead of embracing outsiders, we're starting to become more insular. We need people to open their homes and share their stories and their food now more than ever before.

19

There and Back Again

When Zahabia and I made the decision to get married, I remember one of the first feelings that came over me was relief. I had met, dated and then fallen in love with someone who was willing to marry me, and I was ecstatic. But also relieved. Before I met her so much of my personal and social time was taken over by *looking* for someone— whether it involved friends trying to set me up or meeting dates through Tinder or putting myself out there enough so I attracted the 'right person'. It was quite tiring and I was more than happy to channel all this energy and time into an actual long-term relationship and explore what else it had to offer beyond the short-term benefits.

It is also for this exact reason that I so badly wanted to find an investor for our Series A round of funding. I wanted the introductory emails, presentations, meetings and small talk to end. It was getting in the way of day-to-day operations at TBK. I still recall the number of times I almost had to cancel a catering gig or lost track of important internal meetings, etc., because my mind was completely preoccupied by trying to raise our Series A.

By 2019, the seed round of funding from 2017 had been utilized almost entirely. I remembered a conversation I had had with Lakshmi Pratury, founder of the INK programme and a powerhouse of a woman who has added a great deal of value to my life in more ways than one.

Lakshmi had shared one very compelling piece of advice with me—something I can't help but dispense to a lot of young entrepreneurs that approach me for help. She told me, quite bluntly, that I hadn't raised enough funds!

According to Lakshmi, unless I planned on raising at least US$ 1 million in funding, parting with equity in the company may not have been worth it at all. I had raised about one-seventh that figure, and I didn't think I needed more. More importantly, my company's valuation didn't warrant a million dollars in funding without me apportioning over seventy per cent of it away to investors.

The point of it all evaded me at the time we spoke but when I burned through most of the funding I received within the first eighteen months of scaling and had to immediately plunge into raising a second round while running five outlets, the conversation came back to me in a flash.

As CEO of the company, I had to focus on creating systems, hiring talent and monitoring finances. Fundraising is a job unto itself that demands undivided attention, which is why the first flush of capital has to be enough to take you through at least a couple of years of building your company.

If your valuation leaves you no option but to raise a smaller amount, then borrowing money from friends and family or even an institution and paying interest might make more sense.

Anything less than a million dollars and the entire process isn't worth it. *I should have raised more money,* I thought to myself.

For my first round of funding, I intentionally brought on board multiple investors who were from the industry, believed in the brand and would be willing to guide and advise me. For the next round of funding, Mihir and I were certain we needed a larger institutional investor. By 2019 end, I had personally met at least twenty-five such investors face-to-face and interacted with countless others over the phone or video conference. TBK's popularity and widespread PR always opened doors to conference rooms of the most revered VC funds in the country. Almost every interaction began with the person sitting across the table saying, 'Munaf, I remember reading about you in the ...' or 'Your food looks fantastic!' or 'When are you calling us home?!' It was a great ice-breaker because it immediately gave me the confidence that I needed to floor investors with the pitch that Mihir and I had prepared.

After the initial round of funding, we had grown TBK's sales one hundred per cent year-on-year. By August 2019, we were doing sales of ₹35 lakh per month across four delivery kitchens in Worli, Bandra West, Juhu and Andheri West and a QSR at Kamala Mills. After five years of operations, I finally felt confident about my team, the food and management systems that we had put in place to be able to open and operate twenty delivery outlets across Mumbai and Pune.

I needed another ₹5 crore to do this. Unlike the seed funding pitch, which was earned on passion, great PR and a grand plan for the future, the Series A pitch needed to sell potential investors on sustainability, product differentiation and an exit.

While almost all the investors that I met were sold on the brand, they were concerned about the feasibility of a single-brand, delivery-kitchen model. The general perception among investors in F&B is that, in order to survive in the cloud kitchen industry, you need to have multiple brands representing different price points, flavour profiles, meal segments (lunch, snacks, dinner and breakfast) and maximize use of kitchen square footage and staff. Rebel Foods, with their ten-plus brands and two hundred-plus cloud kitchens across the city, is a glowing example of one such business model.

In an investor meeting with a large family firm based out of Pune, one member of the team questioned me repeatedly about the apparent nicheness of our brand. If you wanted to scale in food delivery, and be profitable, your product offering had to have mass appeal. He believed that by being The 'Bohri' Kitchen we were locking ourselves to a niche market.

I explained to the investor that 'Bohri' food, being half Yemenese and half Gujarati, was actually mainstream in its palatability.

Additionally, our hero item is Biryani, which was among the single-highest-selling food category on Zomato and Swiggy. Lastly, I felt this mix of selling a product which was mainstream, on the back of a brand which was perceived to be niche, was the secret formula to scaling in a cluttered F&B market.

This earned me smiles, praise and even got me a second meeting but the family office chose not to invest for this round.

Another memorable encounter with one of the country's top investment firms included debating my favourite subject—how are you going to compete with the Behrouz Biryanis of the world? Again, a question I got asked a lot, so my response was measured and well-thought-out. I concocted a party trick that went like this: 'What are the three visuals or adjectives that come to mind when I say Behrouz Biryani?' I would ask investors.

I anticipated responses and they typically went like this:
Gorgeous branding
Beautiful photographs
A fictitious war fought in the Middle East over Biryani
Great packaging
Then, I would ask, 'What comes to mind when you think of The Bohri Kitchen?'
Your mom!
A massive thaal
The legendary raan!
The story of how you quit Google to sell samosas
Your famous smoked patti samosas!

My final and follow-up question was, 'What's more memorable?'

While Behrouz was light years ahead of TBK in scale, operations and awareness, TBK definitely had the depth and authenticity. We just needed funds to invest in what we were lacking while continuing to play on our strengths.

Sadly, I could not convince the investors that our business model was capable of squeezing ten to fifteen per cent in net profit per outlet. But the thing about investor interactions is that while you might not always get the money, you do learn a lot.

The very last investor I approached for my second round was an HNI who was looking to make a long-term investment in a food brand that he could work closely with. We crossed paths by complete chance. By the time I was acquainted with him, I had reached the end of my wits and TBK's seed funding.

If I didn't succeed in getting him on board, my core team and I had already worked out a plan on consolidating the business to cut losses. I also had other things on my mind—like marriage. Zahabia and I had set a date for March 2020. I needed the Series A funding or Zahabia and I both needed jobs.

As we inched toward the end of 2019, I was jaded. Yet, this new investor's attitude, history and business philosophy resonated with mine so deeply that my enthusiasm to raise funds was revived. We got along immediately. At the very outset, this investor clarified that he was approaching the business with a view to longevity and sustainability. He felt very strongly about the brand. He respected the very aspects of it that most seasoned investors felt weren't scalable enough—the dining experience, our catering business and pre-orders.

This thinking, however, was at odds with the pitch I was making to him. The investor checked all the boxes when it came to integrity, wisdom and investment size, but he didn't believe in the on-demand business delivery model.

I assumed that perhaps the investor was testing my conviction in the delivery-business model. With someone so interested in the other non-scalable parts of the brand, I drew up an omni-vertical business plan. Yes, I wanted to open a flagship restaurant someday, and yes, I wanted to expand catering and home dining experiences. But home delivery was still very much a huge revenue stream in the short term. It made no sense to pivot from home delivery to, say, a string of QSRs or a restaurant when I had built extensive domain expertise in home delivery. I had spent five years building out our delivery operations. And after four rounds of presenting to this investor and having some amazing conversations with him, he politely backed out of the investment—just like the others. While I did make a friend and possibly customer for life, we didn't get the money!

Now, we were really in a fix. I suddenly found myself in a situation where we needed funds, not to scale, but to sustain our operations. Suddenly from raising funds proactively, overnight I was looking for funding, reactively. A position I had never been in before. Yet—how hard could it be? I had a set of investors, all of them HNIs, who truly believed in the brand and were all completely in-sync with how we had grown the business and our operations. I was sure they would give us the ₹1 crore we needed to buy some time to make the business self-sustaining.

I convinced two of my largest investors on board to infuse another ₹25 lakh. They had one condition—that the other investors pool in the remaining ₹75 lakh. None of the other investors agreed.

While I have a certain amount of clarity on why I was unable to get an institutional investor to put down ₹5 crore, I am still on the fence about what exactly made it difficult for me to raise ₹75 lakh. Perhaps it was the general sentiment towards cloud kitchen delivery and single-brand opportunities or the tanking economy that had people behaving a lot more conservatively with their money. I wondered if it had something to do with the non-vegetarian perception that the brand had in the market. We were known for our Dum Biryanis, raan and Smoked Mutton Kheema Samosas; some of the biggest funds, family offices and HNIs simply don't invest in non-vegetarian food brands[53].

---

53 Note to self. Don't raise funds for a non-vegetarian start-up from an incubator that is run by pure vegetarians.

Ultimately, around December 2019, we had so many balls in the air that juggling everything became impossible. I decided to stop chasing valuations and depending on outside money (partly because I was genuinely fed up with asking people to fund us. Also, because I had no other choice!). During this time, I looked and sounded so distressed all the time that an investor–mentor of mine informed me in his usual jovial manner, 'Munaf, you look like you've been smoked like your mutton samosas!' He made this comment while sitting across from me at a meeting I set up with him to discuss the dire straits both the business and I were in. During the three-hour-long meeting, he told me one thing over and over again—any F&B business that has 'made it big' has been through the exact same struggle I was going through. The answer wasn't to shut shop. I had to make some hard decisions and keep the business afloat in whatever way I could. The tides would turn as would my fortunes.

I took his advice and consolidated the business, shut the new outlets, let go of the central office, let go of more than seventy per cent of our staff[54] and finally brought the business to a point where we were doing half the sale but just about breaking even. Now, we could finally focus

---

54 When I went through this process, I realized that TBK's biggest asset was its people. We had recruited some amazing employees who were sincere, hard-working and genuinely loved the brand despite the eccentric leadership. Letting go of staff was the hardest thing I've done in these five years.

on making a profit and using our own profits to fuel our business growth, at least until investor sentiment improves.

In January 2020, with less than fifteen employees and only Kadir to helm operations and Zahabia to help me with marketing, we readied ourselves to focus on building a self-sustaining business that went back to its roots. The aim would no longer be to send out two hundred boxes of Biryani at an average order value of ₹500 but instead take large ticket pre-orders for family dinners or events. Focus on caterings, our Travelling Thaal concepts. And, of course, our signature Home Dining Experience. Do things which were inherently cash positive and played to the strengths of our cuisine.

If you've watched *The Lord of the Rings*, and even if you haven't, there is a point when Frodo and Sam return to the Shire. They've just had an experience of a lifetime, saving Middle Earth from certain doom and destroying the ring! Yet, when they walk through the Shire, it's as if nothing has changed. No one gives them the hero's welcome they deserve. No one knows what they've accomplished!

I felt somewhat like this in January 2020. I had been on this roller coaster which felt like it lasted a lifetime and something that's become a permanent part of me. Now suddenly, after five years, it felt like I was going back to where it all began.

20

The Final Chapter

Entrepreneurship, by definition, is a marathon of sidestepping, overcoming and sometimes being defeated by the challenges that you face as a business owner. It is what you sign up for when you quit your cushy, well-paying, well-respected job at Google to run a food business.

On 24 March 2020, Prime Minister Narendra Modi ordered a nationwide lockdown because of COVID-19. I chose to suspend TBK's operations, hoping that the lockdown would last a week or maybe two. As I write this almost a year later, in January 2021, we're just about getting back on our feet. What was supposed to be a temporary suspension of services became permanent. We sent our staff home so they could be safe but couldn't afford to bring them back or sustain our kitchen rentals during the lockdown.

As outlet after outlet shut down and operations came to a complete standstill because of COVID-19, I waited to feel gutted, miserable. I had multiple conversations with investors who were nothing but supportive. I started informing my inner circle about the new position TBK was in.

You would think that after living and breathing TBK for five years, finding myself at this juncture would be devastating for me. But it wasn't. I have learnt to not fear failure—what is important to me is to know that I have tried my best. In this case, I knew I had. From spending all my savings to living the life of an antisocial hermit, I had given TBK everything and some more.

My entrepreneurial journey has been studded with setbacks and in every one of those moments I have fantasized about what life would be if I hadn't quit Google.

Strangely, what shook me out of my self-pity was a visit to the Google office.

In January 2020, I took Zahabia to Google's Mumbai office for the first time. It was probably my attempt at giving her that last-mile push to cross the finish line[55], to say—don't be disheartened by my lack of employment or prosperity right now. This is where I came from! I'll find a way to get myself back there.

Walking around the corridors, showing her the fancy meeting rooms, standing desks, infinite snack pantries and table-tennis set-ups, we bumped into an old colleague of mine. Now a very senior member in the Google hierarchy, he joined Zahabia and me for coffee and surprised us with his news. He told us how he planned to delve into

---

55 I got her to sign the marriage contract on 20 March 2020 (three days before the lockdown!).

entrepreneurship with his wife, and that my journey had motivated him to do so!

Riding high on that feeling, we finally caught up with the gentleman who had invited us to the Google office. Vikas Agnihotri, my ex-boss who had played a pivotal role in helping me navigate the decision to become a full-time Chief Eating Officer. He was serving his last month, leaving his position as head of Google India to join Softbank as a partner. I took Vikas through the latest on TBK and the difficult position I was in. To my surprise, it only made his opinion of what I had achieved with my time post-Google even more extraordinary.

This visit made me realize something incredible—that TBK isn't my identity. And while its story is linked to mine, it does not end with me. TBK is now an independent entity of its own. As for me, well, all that I've learnt and gained as Founder and Chief Eating Officer of TBK are things I wouldn't have been able to even imagine doing while working as an employee at any company in the world.

When I quit Google to sell samosas, I wanted to create something that outlived me and in the pursuit of that legacy I chased scale, growth, big valuations and large funding. I had neglected to acknowledge what was already in front of me—the legacy had already been created. Was it making me a lot of money? Not yet. Was TBK going to survive without funding? YES. Had I done something that no one had successfully done before? I think so.

Through this book, I hope to inspire you. I hope to make you laugh a little and I hope that you take away this, if nothing else—if I can do it, so can you.

In June 2020, after three months of paying rents and salaries, without any income, we no longer had the working capital to restart operations. Is this the end of the road for TBK?

I do believe that the brand that we created because of a fight with Mom over a TV remote can survive a global pandemic. After all, #BOHRIFOODCOMA is considered a pretty dangerous affliction by itself.

I MIGHT NOT BE
A BILLIONAIRE,
BUT I KNOW I'VE
ACHIEVED ENOUGH
TO INSPIRE YOU TO
GET OFF YOUR SEAT.

MAYBE REGISTER THAT
DOMAIN NAME YOU'VE
BEEN THINKING ABOUT?

Acknowledgements

Every single like, follower, WhatsApp forward, office lunch conversation, newspaper article, radio mention, any and every instance where someone other than me chose to evangelize The Bohri Kitchen deserves acknowledgement here. Honestly, all I did was make the Facebook page.

Thank you—

Mom & Dad, there aren't enough words to acknowledge the work you have put behind TBK, but I'll try. Thank you for letting me use your talents, your home and endless generosity to get me on the cover of *Forbes India*.

Zahabia Rajkotwala—for choosing to be my life partner, co-author and business partner.

Abdulkadir Kayum (Head of Operations & Investor, TBK)—for believing in the brand and owning it in the same way that I do.

Riyaaz Amlani, Romil Ratra, Rahul Akerkar and Bahram Vakil—I am indebted to you for your invaluable advice and words of encouragement when I needed them the most.

To all my investors, for believing in me and the brand—without you I wouldn't have a story to tell.

Kanishka Gupta, our literary agent—for telling me that I have a story worth publishing.

Sonal Nerurkar, our editor—for handholding us, with immense kindness and patience, on this roller-coaster that is writing a book.

Mihir Mehta, Investment Banker, Ashika Group—for helping me unlock TBK's potential on an Excel sheet and in real life.

Rashmi Uday Singh—for your heart-warming foreword, and for taking Bohra cuisine to the Times Food Awards. Hosting you and Rishi uncle at our home is by far my parents' most precious TBK memory.

To all the journalists who came to our homes with the intention of reporting a paragraph, but left with full-page features on their minds—your stories have helped our food and voice reach more people than I could've ever hoped.

To all my friends for celebrating every small victory bearing my WhatsApp forwards. Thank you for not unsubscribing.

And finally, thank you Google—you taught me that the best company in the world is one which knows when to let you go.

About the Authors

Munaf Kapadia founded The Bohri Kitchen in 2014, before which he used to sell ads at Google, India, and chewing gum at Wrigley's. He's been on the cover of *Forbes India*, is an INK fellow, *Mid-Day* Rising Star Award recipient and winner of the reality TV show *Grilled*.

In his free time, Munaf sails, plays video games and continues to fight with his mother over the TV remote.

Zahabia Rajkotwala is a lawyer by education, marketeer and writer by profession and changemaker at heart. She reads in her spare time and when she's busy. It's a wonder she gets anything else done.

She and Munaf are partners in life and work at The Bohri Kitchen.